Published by Graphis, Inc.

www.graphis.com

ISBN 1-932026-08-8

The Illustrated Voice **Craig Frazier**

Published by Graphis, Inc.

To Suz, Daniele, and Drew

Acknowledgements

I would like to thank my friend Kirk Citron for
encouraging me to do this book in the beginning
and making sure it was done right in the end.

This book, and the work in it, would have never
happened without the unwavering support
and belief from Joni Pon. Thank you.

Thanks to Anne Telford for her editing,
advice, and knowledge of the subject.

I am grateful to Ivan Chermayeff for
his generosity and thoughtful words.
Thanks also to Martin Pedersen,
Milton Glaser, and Kit Hinrichs.

I want to acknowledge these people
for their contributions along the way:
Phoebe Bixler, Bill Creasy, Lance Hidy,
and René Rosso.

Contents

Introduction by Ivan Chermayeff

Craig Frazier: Adding extra. The tired expression "you've seen one, you've seen them all" just doesn't apply to Craig Frazier at all.

Without seeing the body of work, perhaps only having noticed and seen a few images spread out over quite a long time, one might say something along the lines of "I know Craig Frazier's work, he does those drawings of pinheads with hats."

Because the illustrations seen were memorable, attention was paid by those who noticed them particularly because there is always more to a Craig Frazier illustration than a recognizable, individual, personal style. More than the craftsmanship. It goes without saying that the illustrations are made beautifully. Their extraordinary quality lies in the fact that over and over again, an image appears with something extra added. Every drawing has an idea. An idea growing out of the subject. An idea related to the problem that Craig has in hand, which reveals something about it.

Personally, I am very fond of seeing and making images that build on other images and then run a long way. Variations on a theme make each successive variation more than just additive or repetitive. By being one more good thing, they add up geometrically into a body of images that are much more than the sum of their individual accomplishments. One and one is three.

To accomplish this feat Craig Frazier maintains consistently strong, direct, flat forms that seem to be very freshly made. But, judging by the sketches and other indications of the process Craig goes through to produce an illustration, it is not that simple. He uses bright colors for meaning as well as focus. To use his own words, he adds "voice" to his illustrations.

A dramatization of   Beginning November 20   National Endowment
the Tolstoy novel   Made possible by   for the Humanities
presented on PBS-TV   matching grants from   & Mobil Oil Corporation

WAR AND PEACE

Poster for PBS Presentation
by Ivan Chermayeff

I like to think that one of the explanations for Craig Frazier's expressive and memorable illustrations is because he has been, and still is, a designer. The search for a concept, and not putting anything down until a concept is found, is what makes the end product great work that communicates, often about difficult subjects.

To get provocative and meaningful end results requires a grasp of the essential ingredients, knowledge about what they are and the intelligence to exploit them. Scale, surprise, observation, and subtle shifts are the hallmarks of Craig Frazier's illustrations.

He knows what he's doing. The continuous outpouring of excellence is never an accident. On the contrary, Craig Frazier's hard work and intelligence is omnipresent.

—Ivan Chermayeff

This book is a lot about illustration, and a little about design. It is particularly about my own work. Having been a designer for twenty years, I realize that illustration is not the only way to solve a problem. Nor is it the best way in all cases. My approach is not the only approach, or necessarily the best one either. It is, however, the one that I have worked with throughout my career. It is the only one that I understand to any great degree and have any authority to talk about.

The opinions and sentiments in this book are based only on my own experiences so far. They are not researched, tested, or proven. They should be taken as such. I have tried to be uniformly solid in my rationale. There will be points that may make resoundingly good sense and others that appear conspicuously narrow in view.

My illustrations are all crafted by hand and are completely fictional. But beneath the veneer of color and stylization I am always trying to find an approach to communication that is universal and honest. Tapping and reshuffling the viewer's archive of imagery is the big idea. Cutting through, connecting, moving, and making lasting impressions is the job as I see it.

This book is a rearview mirror examination of a body of work produced under an assortment of circumstances. I have attempted to locate and identify the common threads and bring form to an approach I've developed, by the seat of my pants, over time. It has been difficult at times to recall the precise logic that underpinned a particular solution—and uncomfortable at other times to realize that there was no precise logic to recall.

I have tried to remain interesting while factual. I have tried to stick to the story. I have tried to strip the lessons to the core.

This book is pretty much how I see my work. The work is pretty much how I see everything else.

—Craig Frazier

1

Design. The visual microphone.

I have had the good fortune of preceding a career in illustration with a twenty-year career in graphic design. Better still, my first career started before we all used computers—where a triple-ought Rapidograph and a glue pot were the standard tools on our desktops. A time when the sheer effort of crafting our design was so exhaustive that no project ever got developed without a good idea underfoot.

If I've learned one thing, it's that the type of thinking that makes design work well is the same type that makes an illustration work well. They share a common goal: to produce clear and memorable content while employing ample doses of simplicity, wit, and intelligence. Today's most successful illustrators and designers create central themes and maintain respect for the mind of the reader.

The illustrator's work is born, breathes, and thrives in the designer's world. Our illustrations exist in the context of their creative strategies, their words, their clients' influence, and ultimately, their designed pages. To a great extent, the fate of our work rests in the hands of the designer. To survive, it is necessary to be aware and informed of his world and its practice.

Made to read. This poster is all symbols, all inference. The hand is the universal human symbol, the book is the symbol for education and knowledge, and the typography reveals only the partial characters READ. It ironically illustrates how difficult it must be to learn if you cannot read. It was designed for an AIGA poster series on literacy.

12 **Posters.** Symbols at work. Designers have always shared a fondness for symbols. The notion of compacting many words and multiple meanings into a reduced visual form has been around since the appearance of the first hieroglyphic.

When successfully executed, the story told through a symbol instantaneously unfolds into a richer, more encompassing form. It magically prompts us to make a series of visual associations. From that moment on, the content of the symbol stays embedded in its postage-stamp form ready for recall at a single glance. The mind's eye has been activated.

People have a need and an appetite for this sort of thing, and build a lifetime cache of these symbols in their minds for instant retrieval. Aside from the pure pleasure of creating symbols, it is no surprise that designers return tirelessly to this form for messaging. It is also no surprise that corporations continue to rely on them for their inherent branding function.

The challenge with this device is that the meaning of anything symbolic is subjective and always risks misinterpretation. That, coupled with the volume of good and very bad symbols cluttering our culture, makes the work of creating something simple, provocative, and original a daunting task. The seasoned designer learns over time where the jewels are and where they aren't. It takes a deft touch to use the everyday cliché in such a way that it appears fresh, compelling, and, most importantly, memorable.

As much as I believe icons and trademarks are essential in developing a designer's lexicon, the poster is the assignment that never grows old. The lure is always the same. There is nothing quite as satisfying as designing a poster that looks great on the studio wall and reads just as well from across a busy street.

The poster is a place where symbolism thrives and where boldness and simplicity work arm-in-arm. It is home to typography, photography, and, more than anything, illustration. More than any other graphic medium, the "read" of the poster defines its audience, purpose, and ultimately, its success.

The seamless combination of multiple symbols, typography, color, and its public context is the chore of every poster. It is these very elements that torment even the most seasoned designer and give the poster its power and respectability. The journey from thumbnail to full-blown poster never fails to reveal the requirement for a firm grip on so many design principles at once. Recognizing a good poster is one thing—designing one is quite another.

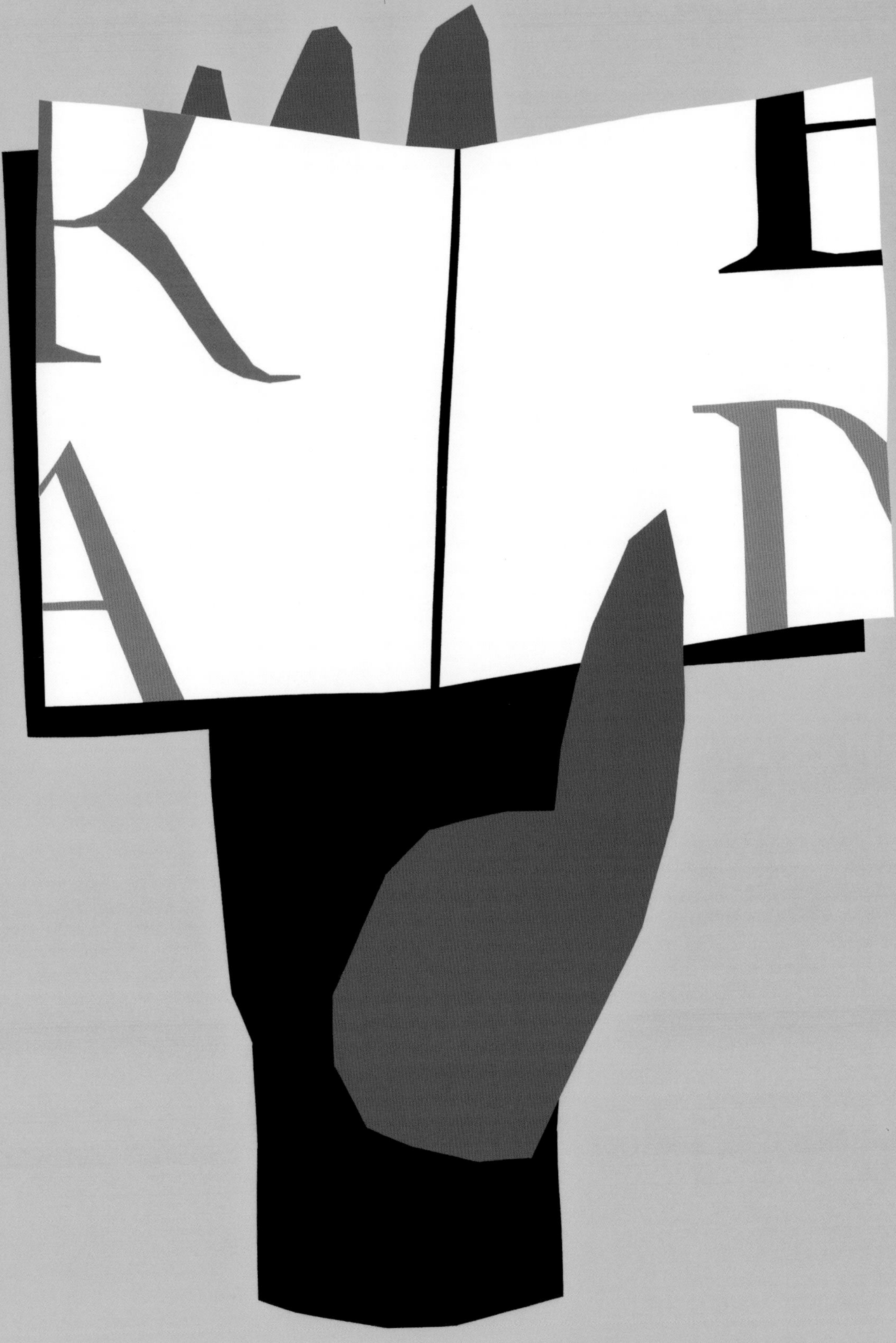

The 1988 World's Most Memorable Poster
Jan 24-Feb 8 Western Merchandise Mart

14

A desirable poster. This was a poster about a poster show. With the title "Most Memorable Poster," I was a little intimidated as to how this poster would measure up. As is often the problem with posters, we get hung up early on what our

work is going to look like rather than what it is going to say. I shifted my attention from the "look" of this poster itself to what the experience of a great poster would be like. This was the message to express. What does admiration look like?

I imagined seeing a beautiful poster and what someone might do to have it. I illustrated what it would look like to arrive after someone had hastily taken the poster. Nothing left but the sheared corners. The absence of the poster piques

our curiosity and prompts us to complete the picture with our image of a memorable poster.

The Mill Valley Film Festival
Oct. 1-11, 1992 Sequoia Theatre

Film stripping. Film festival posters should be entertaining. Like a good movie poster, they need to represent in a moment what you expect to see in hours of motion and sound.

Since no single movie represents the festival, I chose the love story as a classic cinematic theme for the poster. I cast Adam and Eve together in the garden, looking longingly at one other. Because we have seen this image so many times before, we immediately expect to see fig leaves over their privates—thus the zone of interest. I just replaced what we expect to see with something we don't. A simple surprise remakes the long-running marriage of love and film.

Collision of fate. I was asked to design a poster for use in the local high schools to promote safe and sober graduation nights. I agreed, not immediately considering the actual nature of the undertaking.

There may not be a tougher, more cynical audience than a class of seniors which doesn't want a lecture on the perils of alcohol abuse. Designing a poster with the wrong tone meant the possibility of a complete disconnection.

As an experiment in combining symbols, I opted for a very graphic display of the apparent consequences of drinking and driving. Without ever really spelling it out, the poster set up a series of inferences that left the viewer to draw his own conclusions.

I wrote the copy because I felt that at first glimpse the poster might seem attractive before the reality of it set in. It made it to the walls of the seniors' bedrooms and was repurposed as a public service ad in *Newsweek*.

16

Too much fun isn't always a pretty picture. Party safe.

One foot forward. AIDSWalk is an annual fund-raising event in San Francisco. Its purpose is to bring public notice to the ongoing efforts to fight the AIDS epidemic.

As somewhat of a double entendre, I borrowed the ribbon, the well-established AIDS support symbol, and recast it in a new light. In the place of the wing on the messenger Mercury's foot, it assumed the reference of spirit and goodwill. The message is hopeful, moving, and encouraging.

The walk takes place in the city's Golden Gate Park, so I embellished the foot with a garden's thriving foliage.

Sign of the times. My studio is located in the small San Francisco suburb of Mill Valley. It is above a coffee shop and surrounded by various small retail stores.

In the weeks following September 11, I could feel the uncertainty of the store owners and their patrons. No one was quite sure how to act. The merchants didn't know if they should close their stores, and the customers didn't know if they should go in. There was an understandable stalemate happening. No one knew if we could resume any form of normalcy, especially in terms of our day-to-day routines. It was clear that businesses were starting to feel it, especially the small ones.

So I designed a poster. I wanted to give businesses the means to say that they wanted to carry on and fend off this pall of terrorism. They were not closing up under any circumstances, figuratively or literally. It declared a common thread, especially between the mom-and-pop stores and the national franchises.

I printed a hundred posters and offered them to anyone who wanted to post it in their window. In the next week, with the help of a generous printer, we had produced 15,000 posters for the Mayor of San Francisco and the national campaign was launched.

We designed a Web site and over the next few months distributed 200,000 free posters across the country. We created stickers for taxis, banners for rallies, and billboards for the public. It became an unfortunate sign of the times.

AMERICA: OPEN FOR BUSINESS

Cutting the clutter. If you make products for designers, you have to have a trademark that appeals to them. Xaos Tools made software for young designers in the early years of computer design. What was an odd name made for a great graphic opportunity. I designed this dimensional X and convinced the client that however simple, it was perfect for their audience because of its absence of frill and unmistakable "graphicness."

Artificial poster. The rebus is an old and trusted graphic device. Substituting pictures in place of letters, it was a well-suited way of restating the industry acronym for artificial intelligence (AI). Symbolizing the use of technology to imitate the brain's function meant representing the mechanical and the human, a contrast of hard and soft, hot and cold, old and new. The letter was a silver foil stamped, bold condensed "A" with an embossed pattern of circular bumps—kind of like a Braun shaver. The eye was reproduced from an old medical engraving. A lot said with two little symbols.

20

Iconography. The art of reduction. **Just as important to the art of coming up with ideas is the art of whittling them down to their essence. No other graphic expression requires editing like designing icons. Whether it's a trademark, a public symbol, or a glyph— they all count on what isn't there as much as what is.**

Before the advent of the Internet and digital printing, economics dictated that most marks were reproduced monochromatically or at most in two or three colors. Today's corporate vocabulary has grown to include full-color trademarks that often resemble small illustrations rather than symbols. Unfortunately, much of the intrigue and presence of a good mark is lost when rendered so lavishly.

From the days when we drew marks over and over by hand until they were right, I learned that designing symbols and icons is the perfect training ground for learning to think and see symbolically. Its forced economy creates the demand for a simple idea and a sensitive touch when expressing it. It is a practiced eye that knows how much to finish a form to offer enough description—and just how much to omit in order to create its mystery. And it is a practiced hand that knows how to create a lasting form.

The issue here isn't just of graphics, but an issue of time. It's about the time it takes a viewer to see the mark, get interested, solve it, and remember it. If you get it too quickly, it's probably overstated. If you get it too slowly, it's probably too complicated. On the continuum of ordinary to esoteric lies an icon that can attract a reader's attention in seconds and remain in his mind long after.

Mind and machine-the ultimate imagination.

Artificial Intellegence.

Tears for fears. I designed this poster for a campaign that was established shortly after the Columbine incident. I wanted to capture the far-reaching effects of guns beyond the immediate victims; the fact that they cause lifelong sorrow in communities, friends, and families.

In my opinion, the public's sensitivity to the lasting impact of the violence was the key to garnering significant support for the campaign. I attempted to portray that sentiment in a way that was easy to look at and hard to dismiss.

Whenever symbolizing a movement for public aware-ness, it's critical to be clear about the message; in this case—guns are singularly responsible for deaths, enduring pain, and sadness. The poster was never used because the group felt the gun was too prominent.

NATIONAL CAMPAIGN AGAINST YOUTH VIOLENCE

Bird's-eye view. This was a mark designed for a golf course called Eagle Point, which is inhabited by soaring eagles. It's the simple and fluid combination of a golf flag and the bird's silhouette. The nickname for a two-under-par score on a hole, an eagle, is as revered as it is elusive. If you can't have it on your scorecard, it looks nice on your hat.

Hero figure. Designed for George Lucas's computer game company, this mark is part heiroglyph and part logotype. The black L houses two contrasting fonts depicting the science and art of the company. Perched on top is a stick-like figure with arms holding up an arc of rays. All of which form an abstract eye that speaks of the company's creative view of things. Quite possibly one of the most unusual marks I've ever designed, it's still standing strong ten years later.

Nurturing love. This icon was designed to be printed in two colors on envelopes for the US Postal Service. Given the wide-open theme of love, I chose to combine the silhouette of a nurturing gardener with that of a curling, heart-shaped vine. Their snug interdependence seemed to reflect a mutually loving relationship.

Hocus-pocus. Designed for a 3-D computer graphics company named Magico, this mark satisfies our expectations of the name. Using a magic wand and the letter M, it performs an impossible feat by defying our perception of reality. Drawn at a receding angle, the wand enters and impossibly exits the M on the same plane while appearing to "go into" the core of the letter. A mark with its own sleight of hand.

23

Seeing double. The idea of melding two symbols into one is not new to graphic design. Nor is the idea of creating animals out of letters. However, I can say that no other exercise will sharpen one's skills in this department better than creating an alphabet of twenty-six animals as letters and vice versa.

The original letterforms were based on Futura Extra Bold and inked by hand on vellum.

Initially designed as a T-shirt spelling out "The Nature Company," the alphabet was designed to stimulate a child's curiosity with letterforms that resemble animals. The assignment called for the design of only sixteen letters. Unfortunately, the client never printed a production run of the shirts because they felt the art was too graphic. Since I was about two-thirds of the way there, I decided to press on and finish the entire alphabet.

Once I completed it, I designed a children's book and various other products that were distributed to museum bookstores.

The book caught the attention of Adobe, who hired me to redraw the letterforms digitally and capture them as a font. Today, *Critter* is still available as part of the Adobe font library.

M is for **m**ouse,
munching on **m**orsels.

P is for **p**ython,
printed with **p**atterns.

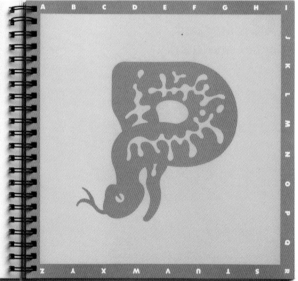

25

Z is for **z**ebra,
zigzagging with **z**eal.

Animal instinct. Like designing twenty-six individual logos, these were a study in visual perception. They each required a perfect balance of animal and letter recognition. There is a split-second chain of impressions that takes place at first read. The animal, then the letter, then the name of the animal starting with the letter. I was constantly checking with my four-year-old daughter to see if what I was seeing was something she saw.

I look back on this experience with great satisfaction. It broadened my understanding of the duality of visual forms, and taught me the meaning of "in the eyes of a child."

As a font, it's easy to create a larger-than-life version of the X, which stands for xenopod, a rare African tree frog.

27

Drawing a better car. In an essay by the director of The Energy Foundation, this annual report spells out the incentives for developing cleaner, more efficient automobiles. Everything from designing electric cars to the impact on our communities was cited and factually substantiated.

I pulled out central messages in the manuscript and proposed a series of graphic storytelling vignettes. Complemented by an editorial-like design and surrounded by white space, the illustrations were packed with symbols and references for a better car. Playful in nature, they serve to gently move the minds of policymakers and concerned citizens to a cleaner place.

Designer and illustrator. The seduction. Though a move from designer to illustrator might look like a backslide down the food chain, I have always felt that it was a pretty natural transition. Creating design and advertising for nearly twenty years has left an indelible thumbprint on my perspective as an illustrator. One can never be too ready for the rigors of the job.

It is highly probable that I could have stayed in my career as a designer and would have been quite happy doing the occasional spot illustration and designing tightly crafted logos. But somewhere in what turned out to be the waning years of my design studio, I discovered the magic and seduction of filling the page with a personal hand-drawn expression.

Two things happened. The first was accidental, when I created the first in a series of little books full of critters made of cut pieces of black masking tape (see page 140). The second was when I designed an annual report for a nonprofit energy foundation and suggested to the client that we use illustration. Since the project was low-budget, I would just draw them myself and save money. They didn't know this was the break I was looking for.

With the completion of both projects, I had been bitten and deeply infected by the illustration bug. I had discovered that a whole world of thinking, dreaming, discovering, and storytelling lay right before me and I had better jump in before the water got too cold again. Best of all, the position required that I do what I had loved to do since I was a kid—draw.

Over the next year or so I managed to illustrate a half-dozen or so of my own projects: brochures, ads, packages, and posters. Each one revealing more about the illustrator's job and its connection to my job as a designer. And each one making the next step easier to take than the last.

Switch to Better Fuels

Whether we hope to reduce oil consumption or tailpipe emissions, it is natural to look at the fuel supply for relief. There is a host of possible alternatives to conventional gasoline, ranging from the close cousins (reformulated gasoline or compressed natural gas) to those more exotic in source but not in use (such as ethanol derived from specially grown crops, called biomass), to those requiring a redesign of the automobile (electric cars or hydrogen fuel cells).

Here, the classic policy dilemma of radical versus incremental reforms becomes apparent: Easy, but small, improvements can be had from moderate shifts to cleaner fossil fuels. Larger contributions will be possible if the nation can stomach the more difficult switch to well-designed biomass programs. And truly revolutionary changes are possible only if automakers begin with a clean sheet of paper.

The last two options on the better-fuels section of our map—electric cars and fuel-cell cars—have captured the attention of air quality officials in California and the Northeast, where air pollution is so bad that almost everyone agrees that big changes are necessary. California has required car manufacturers to sell an increasing fraction of zero-emission vehicles, or ZEVs, beginning with 2 percent of new cars in the state in 1998 (an estimated 31,000 vehicles) and growing to 10 percent by 2003.

Although, in a decade or so, vehicles that run on fuel cells should also become available, in the short run, only electric cars are likely both to be economically viable and to meet the zero-emission standard. The primary limitation of electric cars is the battery, which holds much less energy than gasoline does. This translates into reduced driving range and reduced performance. Against that limitation, electric cars offer reduced maintenance, lower driving costs, higher energy efficiency, quieter operation, and, most important, drastically less pollution. And, as batteries become more effective energy carriers, the problems with range will lessen.

The California regulation promoting electric vehicles has greatly invigorated research and development on electric car technologies in small companies, university labs, and auto manufacturers. There has been a greater advance in control systems, drive components, and batteries in the last three years than in the previous two decades.

But the regulation has also inspired opposition from automakers, who worry they will be compelled to build expensive, poorly performing cars for which there is no market. Electric car advocates note that auto companies used the same arguments against regulations for seat belts, collapsible steering columns, air bags, and fuel-efficiency standards, all of which have been remarkably successful. Auto companies rebut that electric vehicles are a more fundamental change than previous requirements.

The California regulations are clearly steering the economy into uncharted territory: It is too early to predict how zero-emission vehicles will perform or

to gauge their potential market. It is clearly not too early, though, to look for ways to boost the market for electric cars and ensure that society reaps the benefits of this newly invigorated technology. California has started that work by offering a variety of tax incentives for alternative-fuel vehicles. Policy-makers should also consider other ways to make electric cars especially attractive. Cities and states

could, for example, allow operators of electric vehicles to:

- Park for free
- Use high-occupancy vehicle lanes
- Pay reduced tolls
- Receive a tax credit
- Obtain reduced-rate electricity for night-time charging.

Every one of these policies—especially the ZEV mandate—arouses controversy, since they all constitute

some regulatory interference in the market. But the auto itself has impacts beyond the market: Remember the oil crises, the environmental destruction, and the hours spent in congestion. And of course the infrastructure on which the auto depends—highways, streets, and even tax-subsidized mortgages—is built and maintained "beyond the market."

8/9

29

Build Better Cars

During the 1973 oil crisis, policy-makers took a hard look at the nation's energy appetite and found that transportation consumed more than half the nation's oil. New cars averaged only 15 miles per gallon. Despite protests from automakers, Congress passed the Corporate Average Fuel Economy (CAFE) standards, which required automakers to improve that figure to 27.5 miles per gallon by 1988. This policy—which doubled new car-fuel economy—

ultimately resulted in less industry dislocation than Detroit assumed; indeed, it is credited in many quarters with spurring the technological revitalization of the U.S. auto industry. The CAFE law also marks the only success so far in addressing energy use in U.S. automobiles.

What is the potential for extending CAFE standards again, to 55 mpg by 2005? Many independent engineers point to cars on the road that get 50 mpg, and indeed most automakers

have built prototype cars that get more than 100 mpg, without sacrificing performance. Doubling the fuel economy of the nation's fleet would halve its consumption of oil, all but eliminating the need for oil imports.

Automakers have vigorously, and so far successfully, resisted such legislation. They argue that customers want larger cars with more powerful engines, and, barring a boost in gasoline prices, fuel efficiency is just not what customers are looking for. Because legislators are

sensitive to the economic importance of the auto industry and wary of interventions in the market, it is probably fair to say that in the absence of another oil crisis, auto fuel-efficiency standards will stagnate. CAFE worked once, but there is little chance it will be tried again in the near future.

One team of analysts, Amory and Hunter Lovins of Rocky Mountain Institute, argues that a complete reinvention of the automobile is in order, and that only such a thorough redesign can push us beyond the CAFE debate. Their concepts, described in the box opposite, should lead to cars

that get more than 100 mpg, with drastically reduced pollution, noise, and required maintenance. If such "hypercars" were developed, their non-fuel attributes—safety, reliability, nimbleness, and lower cost—could induce customer demand. The fuel savings would be a free byproduct.

Moving toward the "hypercar." On Sept. 29, 1993, the Big Three automakers committed to developing a triple-efficiency "clean car" prototype within a decade. A really efficient car, however, can't be made by pursuing incremental refinements to a fundamentally obsolete concept of the automobile. A leapfrog is needed, is now feasible, and can far surpass the 1993 goal. Striking technological innovations have been made that, artfully integrated, can yield safe, affordable and otherwise superior cars getting hundreds of miles per gallon.

Accelerating today's heavy steel cars requires engines so large that their efficiency is halved: only 15-20 percent of the gasoline's energy is available to move the car, and only 1 percent available to move the driver. Almost all of the lost power heats the tires and road, the brakes, and the air pushed aside by the car.

The key to the super-efficient "hypercar" is first to make it ultralight. Advanced composite materials can cut total weight three- to fourfold while improving safety. Sleeker streamlining can cut aerodynamic drag while better tires and lowered

weight will reduce tire and road loss. Once this ultralight strategy has largely eliminated unrecoverable energy losses, the remaining loss of wheelpower is braking. But if the wheels are driven by special electric motors, those motors can act as electronic brakes that convert motion back into useful electricity.

A long driving range can then be achieved by burning any liquid or gaseous fuel, in a tiny onboard engine or other powerplant, to make electricity to run the wheel-motors. A few batteries can temporarily store and reuse recovered braking energy. This "hybrid" technology combines the best of gasoline and electric cars.

Combining these approaches yields extraordinary synergies. Adding hybrid-electric drive to an ordinary production car increases its efficiency by one-third to one-half. Making an ordinary car ultralight doubles its efficiency. But doing both together can boost a car's efficiency by about tenfold.

Amory B. and L. Hunter Lovins
Rocky Mountain Institute

6/7

*L*ISTENING:

the KEY *to*

SUCCESSFULLY ROUTING *a* PROBLEM

TOWARD *its*

RIGHTFUL SOLUTION.

Blind faith. A brochure for Oracle Computer's Technical Support group, the content was dry and technical and in need of a more humanized presentation.

Early in the project I wrote single lines for each spread summarizing and identifying central messages. I presented that copy along with sketches to the client to get approval for the design direction.

I had not intended to do the illustrations myself, but with the client's immediate approval I saw no reason to hesitate. Though very much "early work," these illustrations were already a starting point for characteristics I employ today.

It was after the piece was produced that I realized that the "ear tree" I had drawn bore a resemblance to a poster that Milton Glaser had done years before for the Academy of Recording Arts and Sciences. My illustration was quite different and not nearly as beautiful, but my apologies nonetheless to Milton.

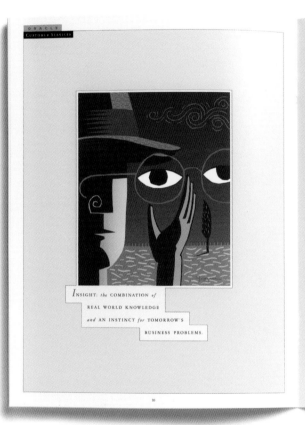

Full service. This was an annual report for the then–young Symantec Corporation. The theme of the book was the emergence of computer connectivity and home computing.

Working with the writer, we developed a direction that had wonderfully illustratable copy.

Lines like "welcome to the neighborhood" and "one way to look at many ways to connect." It expressed new, yet conceivable concepts about the future of computing. The tone was refreshingly clear.

I presented black-and-white comps complete with proposed headlines and illustration ideas. I finished one of the illustrations to show them how graphic and simple the book would look—like the ideas they were promoting.

Concerned that the client might be suspicious of the designer hiring himself to do the illustrations, I didn't reveal the illustrator. Once they expressed their approval of the direction, I let them know that I would go right to work on finishing the illustrations.

It remains a favorite piece of mine for its overall simplicity.

32

In the past 12 months, we put network administrators in their proper place: at the center of things.

2   12 SYMANTEC CORPORATION

Welcome to the neighborhood.

After 20 years, the personal computer has finally come home.

From its debut as a hobbyist machine in the circles of a few dedicated enthusiasts to its ultimate integration into corporate America, the humble PC has profoundly changed the way most of us think and work. And now, with an estimated 33%[1] of U.S. households owning one or more of these machines, the PC is finally beginning to make its mark on the folks down the street.

At Symantec, we've been with the PC virtually from the start, supplying productivity, communication, and utility software to help users get the most from their computers. Our heritage as a PC software developer has always encompassed an intimate knowledge of desktop users, and of the kinds of tools they need to keep their systems working at peak efficiency. Today, as the computer comes home to a broader audience, we're leveraging this knowledge to help these new users feel more comfortable with, and in better control of, their computing experiences.

To this end, Symantec in fiscal 1996 invested heavily in developing marketing activities that addressed the specific concerns of new users. We initiated, for example, a highly successful program that communicated through mainstream consumer and business media basic tips and techniques for home PC operation and maintenance. Just as we know we should change our car's oil every 3,000 miles, we also should know about certain techniques—such as backing up files and protecting against viruses—that keep our computers and data in optimum shape.

This is especially true as the emergence of the Internet offers new ways to transmit not only data, but also, unfortunately, viruses. Although we may be vigilant ourselves, we still need to practice "defensive computing" in our daily lives. Symantec's Peter Norton Group has been at the forefront of the Company's effort in this area, with our industry-leading *Norton Utilities* and *Norton AntiVirus* products. These powerful programs enable users to perform basic diagnostic and repair functions through simple, unintimidating interfaces that shield users from complex, underlying operations. With 70%[2] of the U.S. market, and 53%[2] of the market outside the U.S., *Norton AntiVirus* is the program of choice in the anti-virus category, as is *Norton Utilities* in the broader utilities category.

Through ongoing enhancements in these and other utility programs, Symantec will continue to ensure that the Company's products remain synonymous with the needs of basic, everyday computing. Welcome home.

1. Computer Intelligence InfoCorp, January 1996
2. International Data Corporation, 1995

It's not just for business anymore; the PC is now at home anywhere. And so is Symantec software.

www.growth.explosive

Ten years ago, the typical information repository was a small drive on a user's desk. Today, thanks to the Internet, it is virtually the entire universe.

Unlike companies that are merely riding the current Internet wave, Symantec continues to be an integral part of it. In fiscal 1996, we were active on several online fronts, perhaps none more significant than our efforts to bring forth *Symantec Café*, the first Windows-based integrated development environment devoted exclusively to Sun Microsystem's Java programming language.

Based on our award-winning *Symantec C++* development environment, *Symantec Café*—our visual Java development and debugging tools—provides substantial enhancements to Sun's Java Development Kit. With *Café*, programmers can create programs that add interactivity to their Web pages. Or, they can create standalone applications such as corporate Intranet pages that can then be delivered to any Java-supported environment without recompilation.

Café's platform independence, along with the ability of Java applications to communicate over the Internet, has created an explosion of interest on the part of active developers on all platforms. In recognition of the huge proportion of Web development performed on the Macintosh, the Company in April 1996 introduced *Symantec Café* for Macintosh.

The growing popularity of the World Wide Web has, however, been accompanied by an increase in the infection rate of client systems from viruses traveling over the Internet. To address this, the latest version of our Norton AntiVirus software will offer free, automatic virus updates over the Internet. Additionally, our Symantec AntiVirus Research Center has developed the first native-Java virus scanner for Java applets sent over the Internet, as well as an in-house automation technology that can be used to analyze, replicate, detect, and define a large subset of the most common computer viruses.

The new Web platform also represents a significant opportunity for Symantec in the emerging area of online software distribution. Although we will not see the end of the retail package anytime soon, more and more customers are demanding the ability to purchase software directly over the Internet. With our expertise in distributing utilities over networks, we are well positioned to provide the products and services, such as automatic updating, that will enable and enhance this new capability.

In the near future, we expect most Symantec products to have a Web-based component to facilitate their smooth integration into this new medium. Until then, we will continue to set the pace not only in online development, but also in helping to define the new dynamics of personal computing.

The message is the medium, and Symantec is helping people write it.

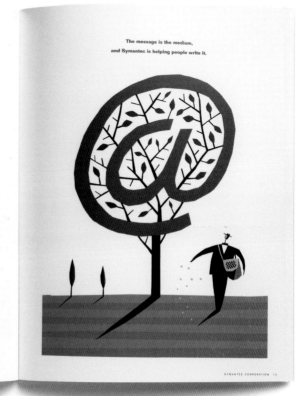

34

2

Content. Drawing for meaning.
Most illustrators have a fondness for drawing, and given the choice would rather draw than do almost anything else. The illustrator's real work isn't usually the drawing part, but the thinking part. Because without relevant content in our work, it doesn't get the job done.

I have found it to be an incomplete exercise to try to produce good work solely on the merits of its appearance. It is a deeper and more rewarding practice to consider the meaning of an illustration as the benchmark for its success. This requires the examination of our work in the context of the reactions it sets off in the minds of its viewers. In a sense, it is drawing with one eye on our work and the other on its cause and effect.

With that in mind, I have found that the best art direction isn't directing what the illustration will look like, but what it will say. The first job is a drawing exercise, the second a charter to participate in the forming of a visual voice—a far more demanding and fulfilling job. The engagement and mental conversation with the viewer becomes the real task of the illustration. And its ability to fortify a client's message is the measure of its influence.

36

Sketching. Before the idea gets away. The sketch-book is a treasured friend for those of us in the idea business. It is a repository, an archive, a scrapbook, a safe haven for musings. It is a place to put specific thoughts, loose ramblings, fleeting notions, doodles, and incomplete visual ruminations. It is a reminder that there are always blank pages ahead awaiting fresh ink and your mind will be freer if you just fill them. It is also a reminder of places and times, and of particular streams of consciousness that only you can decode. A sketchbook serves you at the moment when the idea runs the risk of slipping away if not captured by your pen. And it serves you over time as a record of your conscious and unconscious visual deliberations.

Occasionally, I sketch my surroundings, usually while on vacation, but my sketchbook is typically used for work. I find it to be a welcome place to begin to think about a particular problem. I like to take it to lunch with me and draw thumbnails while I read a manu-script for an assignment. It tends to be full of lots of very bad sketches—both technically and conceptually. To that end, it serves a valuable purpose. It is a place where there are no clients, no critics, and no onlook-ers. A place where anything goes, and judgment is not a regular participant. If I am lucky enough to stumble onto a good idea between the pages, it will graduate from the sketchbook to a fresh piece of tissue paper and maybe even turn into a finished illustration.

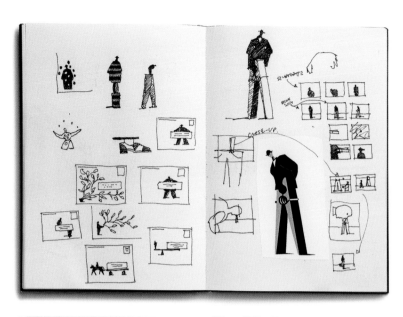

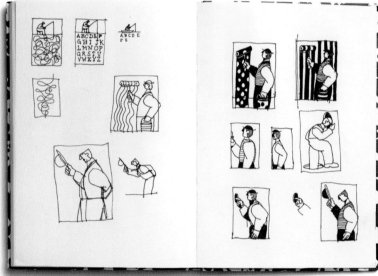

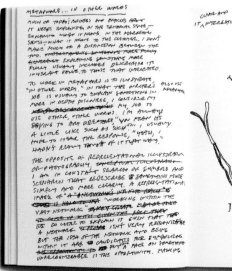

38

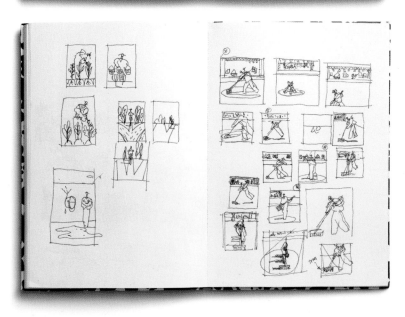

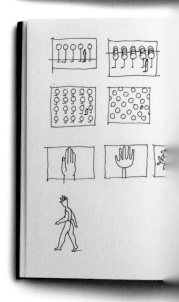

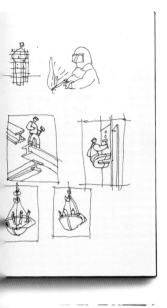

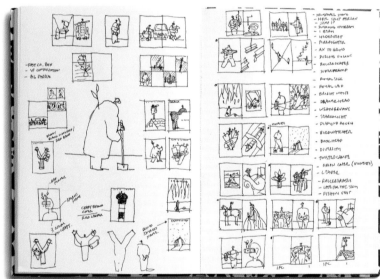

39

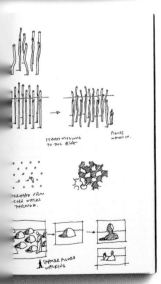

Safety in numbers. As much as I know it's possible that a problem can be solved on the first sketch, I'm sure that a few more will improve the odds. And because I also know that there are several solutions to any given problem, I do a lot of sketching.

If not sketching in my sketchbook, I use a tissue pad. I always have. Tissue makes sketching a completely iterative process. The ability to retrace a drawing takes the onus off any sketch having to be the perfect one. In fact, I purposely try to "load up" the page in the hopes that some kind of chemical reaction will take place.

Unless I'm on a really tight deadline, I consciously let myself meander around the page with little ideas trying to spawn more little ideas. Occasionally, I do see an image in my mind before I draw it and the process is condensed. But typically, this form of visual note-taking leads me down an unpredictable yet revealing path. As in my sketchbooks, I do lots of poor sketches with no real concern for the drawing's execution. I'm literally looking for an idea to show itself before I invest in its composition. I usually know it when I see it.

Before I show the client the sketches, the composition is pretty well worked out. I do one last sketch with a fresh pen and fax it off to them. Once they make their selection, I redraw it once or twice again to make final refinements.

I keep all of my tissues and page through them regularly, looking for remnants and spare parts that help get the motor running.

40

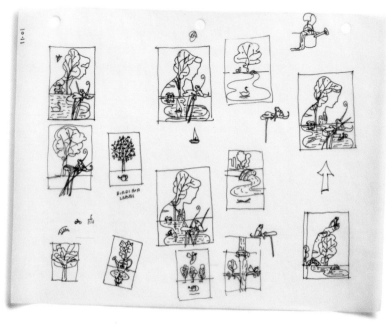

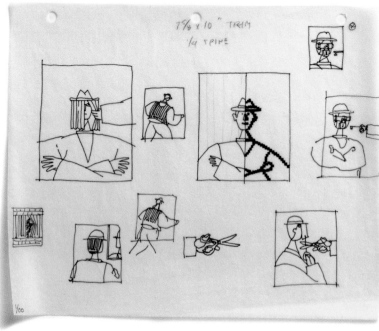

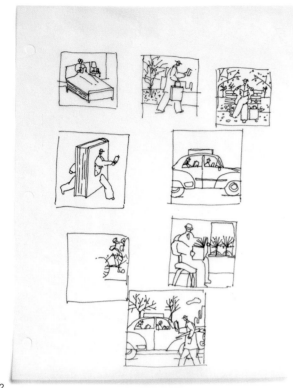

42

45

Swimming upstream. Regularly my assignment briefs set out to describe how distinct the company's practices are from their competitors. In this case, the client was an investment firm who wanted to convey that their approach to investing was slightly unconventional. My job was to bring new reference to the notion of an alternative method of going about things.

I was hoping not to see the illustration rooted in the typical financial vernacular. Swimming against the current occurred to me and led to the sketches for the direction I would ultimately take.

The intrigue in this illustration is the relationship between the classic business-suited figure in silhouette and the swimmer appearing to be almost passing through him. Though the figures appear to conflict with one another, the perfect fit of the swimmer's leg and shoulder with the other figure's arms creates a particular harmony that makes their relationship almost natural.

Beauty and the beast. I was asked to illustrate an article on breast cancer for Hermann Hospital's magazine. The article was primarily informative, discussing the disease from symptoms to procedures to recovery. It also described a woman's vulnerability to the disease and particularly the emotional fallout from a mastectomy. Not an easy subject to illustrate.

I thought that, at least, I could illustrate the physical issue, and at most, approach the emotional angle of the issue. In any case, I didn't want it to appear as a male's narrow study of the problem.

I started with a simple view of a woman's body. I knew that I needed to characterize the woman in such a manner to avoid getting caught up in size of breasts, age, and ethnicity

(thus the blue figure). I also knew that I wanted to be as symbolic as possible, with ample room for interpretation and little room for misinterpretation. I felt that if I could imply the risk of the disease, I would have done a good job.

My first sketches started placing her hands in a nurturing and protective position. I felt that it was too obvious and really didn't indicate the threat.

However, at that moment, I saw the implied X that led me to draw the crossed roses.

Though I think it must have been intuitive at the time, the roses were both beautiful and deadly, their thorny intersection marking the spot. Both the figure and the roses are beautiful at first glimpse, but then another message unfolds.

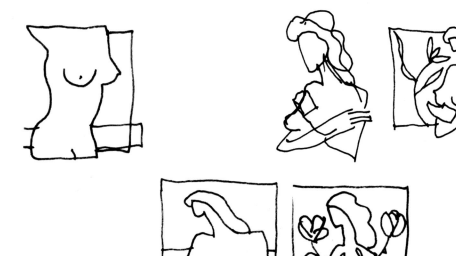

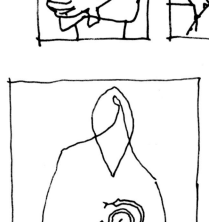

The idea. The heart of the matter. "That's a good idea, let's do that." We hear it said almost every day. We say it ourselves with frequency. It's the response to a proposed plan of attack, like what we're going to have for dinner, or which movie we are going to see. It's an immediate confirmation that our thinking has registered with someone else. A signal that our influence has reached out past the confines of our own mind and into another's—and is accepted.

For the little things in life, the response comes quickly. For the bigger things like "I think we should paint the house pink," the response comes slower. As visual inventors, we constantly run up against the possibility of getting the "pink house" reaction from our clients. It may also be followed by the words, "I don't think I like that idea."

It's clear to me that the reception of our ideas has as much to do with a client's orientation to them as it does with their quality. If we hadn't been considering painting the house, and hadn't examined what might be involved, it's unlikely that immediate agreement to the suggestion of pink is going to happen. On the other hand, if we had been looking at other houses and thinking generally about the nature of the problem, we might greet the idea with a more informed and favorable response.

If we aren't in the mood for ideas, we aren't likely to take to them very positively. If we don't know what we are trying to solve, it's hard to objectively evaluate the possibilities. That goes for the illustrator as well as the client.

Ideas are an indispensible ingredient in creating an illustrated voice. Without them, we have little foundation in telling a story that will arrest anyone's attention for more than a second. It's the idea that draws the viewer beyond the surface of the page. It's the idea that establishes the premise for the conversation. It's the idea that rescues us from our tendency to think along dangerously straight and ordinary lines. It's the idea that moves us.

If an illustration has a central idea, it offers more to assess than simply its subjective features. The response "I don't like it" isn't enough if the illustration has an idea that can be examined. It doesn't mean it will be accepted just because it has one, but with an intellectual basis, our work becomes much more receptive to objective evaluation. Working in ideas gives us a meter to judge the merit of our solutions. We begin to look for answers inside the heart of our drawings. With practice, we can't help but produce more meaningful illustrations.

Our yearning for purposeful ideas is an addictive appetite that requires regular feeding and constant affirmation. Concurrent with our responsibility to make new ideas is our role in inspiring a forum for informed judgment—so that unfamiliarity isn't the cause for rejection. In the end, it's the only way we are going to paint the house pink.

More power. Every company wants more power in one way or another. In the competitive world, nothing is better than invisible power. I had both of these ideas at an early sketch stage on an assignment (target sketch on previous page). The prop supplying the most obvious mechanical power and the enlarged target created a kind of strategic power. The client selected the prop idea and I later finished the target idea for another client.

The prop illustration is a perfect example of the power of scale in a graphic sense. The prop is most prominent, not only due to its relative size, but its blade's red highlights break right through the cool blue water. In developing the idea, I reduced the size of the boat, and, of course, improved the design of the blades themselves. I removed the fish because he looked headed for trouble.

Improved chances. This is one of those "what if this were real" scenarios, the idea being how to elegantly improve our odds. Conceptually it makes sense: bigger target, better chances. Visually, it's a trick that we are willing to go along with. By encircling the distant target with an "O" held in the foreground, the character essentially flattens the planes and eliminates the distance between the two. Not only is the target bigger, but now it is right in front of us.

50

PRODUCTIVITY

Making progress. For an article in *Business Week*, the message was that productivity was on the rise among small businesses. When I think of productivity, I think of the mechanics of actually making something. Even though it's the dirty workings of a lot of businesses, the graphicness of the assembly line makes for a simple and strong symbol.

I started by sketching mechanical assemblies that moved in an upward direction and realized that the classic assembly line was probably the right symbol. The concept was that they were making arrows— a simple expression for making something positive.

In the final illustration, I edited out the incoming pieces and outgoing arrows. I thought they cluttered up the floor, and were unnecessary distractions.

I think this illustration speaks well for the growing cheese industry.

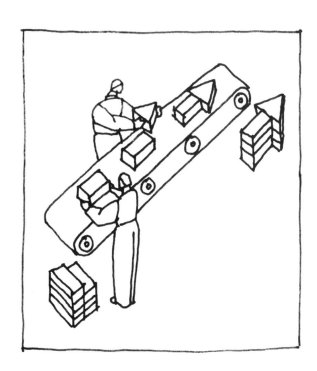

53

Digital reading. This was a feature article in *Time* magazine about the advent of digital books, a narrative on the progress of capturing books for reading on the computer. It was a pretty simple concept to grasp, which meant the illustration needed to be that much more intriguing.

It needed to portray more than just a picture of text on a computer screen, because the real breakthrough was the ability to capture books and present them in a fashion that mimics the way we read them.

This notion described the union of two very different worlds. Just the kind of situation that makes an interesting illustration.

I typically don't like to draw computers because they are so overused as a symbol for technology. In this case, the story hinged on the physical nature of a computer and our interface with it. A simplified laptop said just enough. A reader was also a critical element in this high-tech promise.

The job was essentially to create the romantic idea that the book was "within" the computer, not just on it. By floating the computer, I liberated the illustration from reality and was able to design it more as a visual equation.

It took a few attempts to find the right intersection of the book and the computer. The final composition presents a conceptual revelation of what is now available to the reader on his computer.

I subconsciously borrowed from another drawing about reading I had done previously. (page 78). The two are both similar and very different.

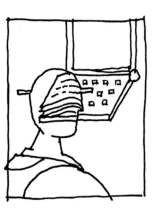

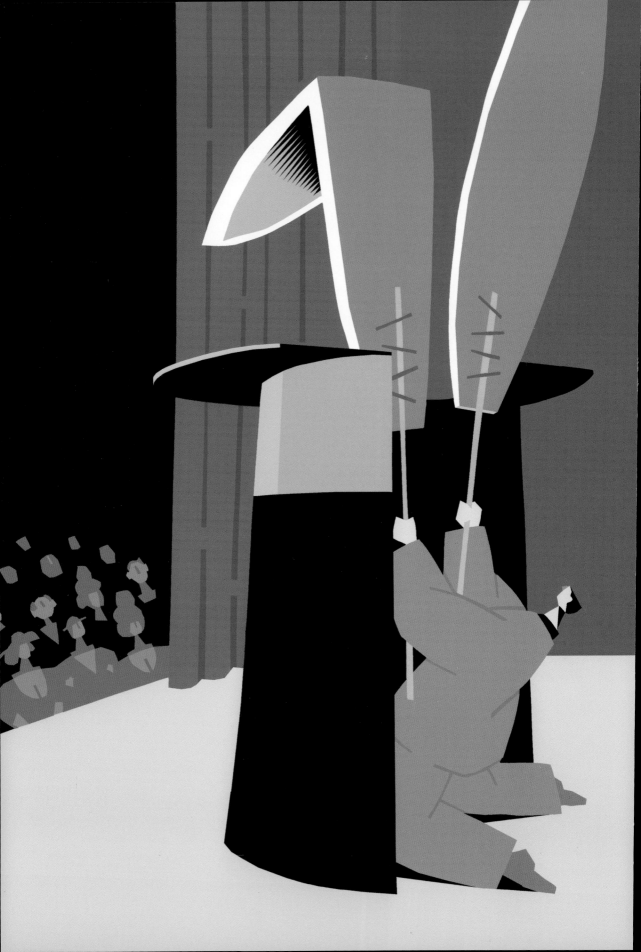

Backstage pass. I'm always interested in creating an alternative view of things. In fact, I probably use this technique more often than any other in my work.

It's not as much an illustration technique as it is psychological. Most of the time we are trying to convince our readers of something that they either know nothing about or already have preconceptions about. In either case, I find it helpful to present them with a fresh perspective that may serve to jar, or even change, their existing perception. With the right dose of humor and wit, even the most stubborn can be enlightened.

Just before the burst of the dot.com bubble, *Red Herring* magazine featured a story predicting the collapse of the venture capitalist community. Its angle was to lift the veil and expose a cynical and humbling view of their business practices. It reminded me of the man behind the curtain in *The Wizard of Oz*.

It was really about an illusion that everyone had been believing until now. So I started exploring the old rabbit-in-the-hat trick. I wanted to create an inside view to a trick on the edge of failure. I decided to take the viewer backstage and reveal the protagonist's struggle to uphold his performance.

Adapting the three-quarter perspective of the situation both broadened our view and gave me several little graphic opportunities.

The depiction of every tiny element becomes critical to the total feel of the illustration. This piece is more involved than many of mine and had the potential of getting "overdrawn" very quickly. Because I draw these fairly small, I am forced to limit the detail I can employ.

The curtain is as simple as possible, the rabbit ears appear almost stapled to the sticks, and the audience is rendered monochromatically.

I wrestled with the coloring in this piece and settled with these four dominant panels of color. The black theater, red drape, blue wall, and beige stage play against one another to create depth and a backdrop for the hat, ears, and figure. The boldness of those panels lend tremendous attention to little spots of color like his hat, the sticks, and the staples.

I think my favorite part of the piece is the falling pink ear that gives us a hint of what the audience is seeing. If they could only see what *we* see.

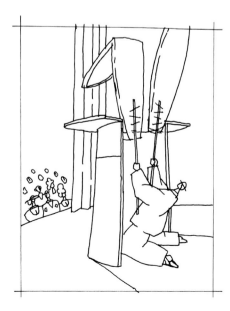

Arms around the problem. The Orion Capital Annual Report needed a way to discuss the subject of growing their niche businesses. More importantly, it needed to humanize the otherwise abstract activity. Their distinction was that the company was not just careful, but nurturing, in selecting its candidates. The writer wrote the final headline after I submitted the finished illustration.

58

Words and pictures. Speaking in harmony. Since most illustrations appear on a page adjacent to related words, it stands to reason that the two should coexist in the service of a larger and common goal. An illustration's success depends on how well it reflects, characterizes, supports, and even explains the words that share its space.

Words are the kindling under an illustration's fire. They are a starting point, a seed for thinking. They are the vehicle for a message in its most literal and comprehensible form. They are what the illustration sums up—what it expands. Words are the touchstones for an illustrator's visual leaps of faith. They are the currency that connects an illustration's story to a practical and tangible purpose.

Words come in many fashions. Designers like to use tiny, promising headlines. Advertising art directors like to use clever medium-size headlines, and editorial art directors like to use short, big headlines followed by smaller subheads that restate those headlines. And writers like their words to be read. Of course I'm satirizing, but the point is that everyone views their words a little differently.

The reality is that the words are often the most difficult part of getting an assignment off the ground. I have learned over time that the writing tends to speak a lot about a designer's approach and ability to zoom in on concise notions. Just like the other facets of design, the style of writing and its treatment on the page signal the tone the piece will take.

I carefully study a project's brief before accepting an assignment, to evaluate if there is going to be a comfortable relationship between the writing and the illustration. I'm looking for content as well as the specific points that need communicating. I'm looking for messages I'm interested in drawing.

The ultimate goal is a complementary relationship between word and image—each serving to better explain the other. And the combined effort speaking more eloquently than the individual parts.

Skillfully selecting successful markets.

Model behavior. I wanted to draw a timeless problem that anyone can identify with and the leaky boat fit the bill. It was perfect, because I could show without tragic consequence the annoying interruption a leak can cause to an otherwise peaceful row on the lake. After drawing the incoming leak, the solution presented itself.

Though essentially a visual prank, the illustration demonstrated how obvious solutions appear if looked at from another perspective.

UNDERSTANDING PROBLEMS
CREATES SOLUTIONS.

THE SOLUTION IS OFTEN
FOUND IN A CLEAR UNDERSTANDING
OF THE PROBLEM.

Solutions lie at the heart of the problem.

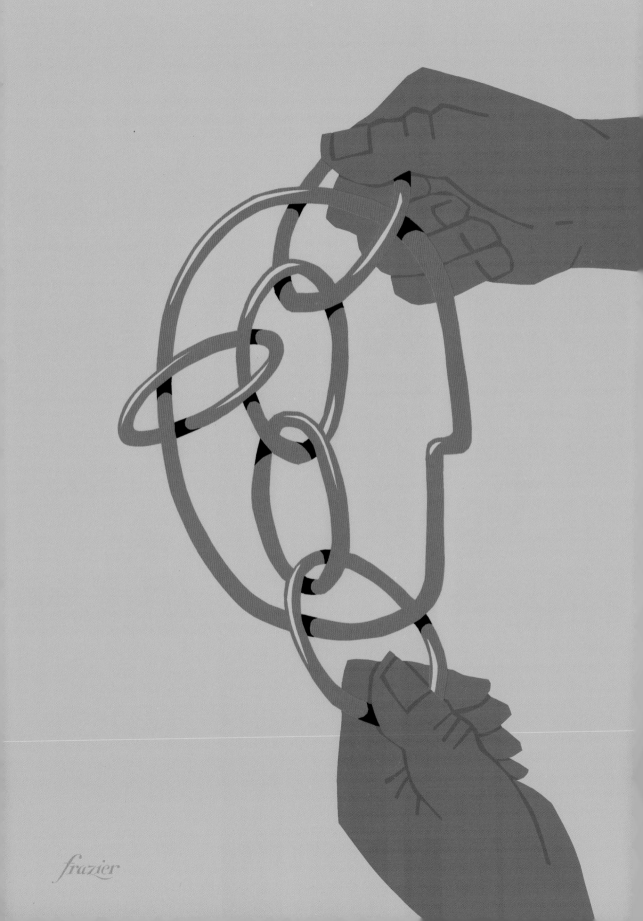

frazier

Leadership school. In an article in the *Yale Alumni* magazine, the author tells of a graduate course in which students are trained to become leaders by developing their habits of thinking in grand strategic terms.

Titled "Training the Next Leaders," the article described the rigorous exercises that students are put through to build their mind and their character to withstand the demands of leadership in all forms.

Because I was given two illustrations to explain the article, I was able to split the messages, "strategic thinking" and "training." The "human puzzle" suggests that leaders are adept at sorting out the complex variables that compose problems. The "high bar" suggests the lofty standards students must set for themselves in order to achieve leadership potential.

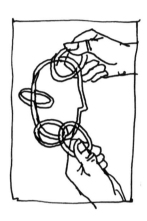

65

Personal book. Designed as an elegant keepsake for the 3Com Corporation sales staff, this little book spells out the company mantra and how to put it to work. The opening spread claims "This book is for you." Initially, I saw a figure walking proudly with his rule-book firmly in hand. Knowing that wasn't much of an idea, I made the same book bigger than life and integrated it within the figure itself. A sure sign that it was taken seriously.

66

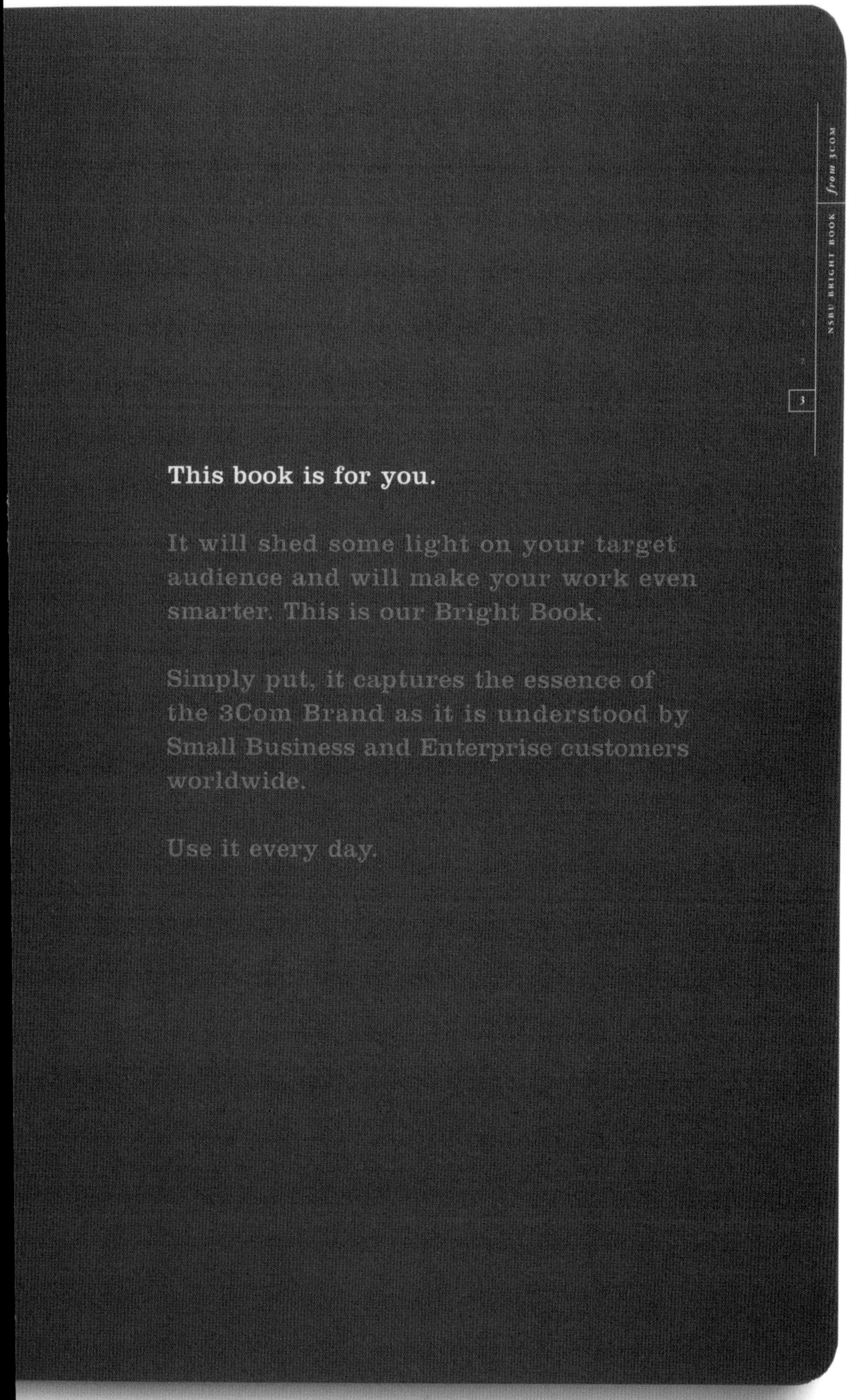

NSBU BRIGHT BOOK *from 3COM*

3

This book is for you.

It will shed some light on your target
audience and will make your work even
smarter. This is our Bright Book.

Simply put, it captures the essence of
the 3Com Brand as it is understood by
Small Business and Enterprise customers
worldwide.

Use it every day.

67

The right angle. This is an article opener for *Harvard Business Review* called "The growth crisis and how to escape it." The subject was that growth is getting tougher to sustain in the present economy, and executives are stymied using traditional tactics to deal with the situation.

This "trappings of success" story cites a series of "hidden assets" that companies are sitting on that can effectively produce growth. An insightful look at revelations that are right beneath their feet.

I wanted to illustrate the sense that big solutions are often a function of thinking narrowly about the problem. That problem-solving is as much about resourcefulness as it is measured thinking.

The idea of getting water to the top of the towering hedge, and seeing over at the same time, was simply a matter of reengineering the immediately-available tools.

68 **Wit.** The conversation starter. If I could only use one tool in addition to a pen, I would have to choose wit. That's not to say that beauty and subject matter aren't important, but it is wit that sets the synapses firing in our heads and requires us to cognitively digest the things we see. It is the stuff that calls our minds to active duty and reminds us that there is definitely more to the picture than meets the eye.

On an immediate level we think of wit as clever and humorous. Like seeing the banana peel that the pedestrian is about to slip on. But on a more developed level, we see wit in forms that resemble visual riddles, or incongruities that intrigue us and bear investigation. It's putting objects in places they don't belong, casting shadows into forms they don't resemble, exchanging what we expect to see with something contradictory, or stopping time at a moment that beckons us to predict the outcome in our heads. Illustrated wit makes the difference in a visual monologue and a dialogue.

The urge to incorporate wit in my work is out of appreciation for it everywhere else in my life. I love to laugh and I love the satisfaction of feeling included in the repartee. It seems to reoccur as a basis for the best friendships and a key ingredient in meaningful conversation. It is a character trait I like in people that indicates not only their appreciation for the lighter side of things, but their ability to exchange ideas with a sense of intellectual playfulness. It's playfulness in the most positive sense of the word—where the fun is genuine, mutual, and always stimulating.

Ironically, wit becomes a more viable approach the more serious the context. It's very rare that I get an assignment that strikes me as humorous upon initial reading. In fact, many are painfully solemn. It's usually those very jobs that require the illustration to transport the reader to a place the words can't do alone. Thank goodness for wit.

There is no short answer for convincing the nervous client about the intrinsic merits of wit or whether a particular illustration will pass the test or not. I never attempt to second-guess a client or their audience. Nor do I overstate the obvious just to make extra sure they get it. I generally rely on my own sense of what is witty for guidance. Drawings that take the least amount of explaining are usually on track and those that take the most explaining usually aren't. It ultimately amounts to a practiced intuition, a willing client, and a belief that people are smarter than you think.

Almost smart. In an editorial in *Red Herring*, the author paints a skeptical picture about the future of artificial intelligence. He describes the fact that however advanced its promoters say it is, it still can't imitate the basic function the brain performs in solving complex problems. It is reckoning day for the technology's future because investors are unwilling to continue to fund the apparently empty promise.

The situation was ironic. Here is a technology that is on the edge of a breakthrough, but can't figure out how to solve its own riddle. If it were a little smarter, it could get a little smarter.

I wanted to portray this as a moment in time where the technology comes to terms with itself. In the well sketch I was posing the question of how full or empty is was. In the figure sketch, which was selected, it was more of a concerned moment of reflection, it's as if to say, like the scarecrow in *The Wizard of Oz,* "if I only had a brain."

Altered states. These illustrations were both done early in my illustration career and sparked my interest in drawing visual contradictions.

Both of them were designed to express a consulting firm's affinity for discovering their clients' not-so-obvious business opportunities.

One illustration finds the character standing alone pondering the brick structure around him. He is perhaps sensing that he is in the middle of a bigger picture, a picture that can only be seen from our vantage point.

The other illustration was lucky happenstance. I drew this first with the horizon straight and while staring at it, I suddenly saw the possibility of rotating the scene inside the wheel. With that slight alteration, the reality is completely changed and anything becomes possible. It's that simple.

74

Coming attraction. The *Los Angeles Times* was doing a story on the new and improved L.A. Film Festival. Nothing was especially visual about it other than the ambition to make it into a world-class event.

Lured by the romance of movies and their iconography, I soon found myself groping for a fresh take on an old subject.

As is often the case, the story lacked a strong point of view which caused me to wrestle to make connections.

Wanting to make use of the near-perfect graphic of a film strip, I was fearful of falling into a "wasteful abuse of a classic icon." I was already no stranger to it (see page 15).

After a few failed attempts

at depicting the inside of the festival, I backed off and decided to look at the fanaticism and style surrounding it, the pomp and circumstance of the festival.

Clad in a mile of film, this fan awaits a movie's debut with the strong hope of being spotted—both good reasons to attend.

Secret weapons. This is a sister to an illustration I show on page 153. The task was to claim the positive merits of a group of partners without appearing boastful.

Because people's strengths in business tend to be experiential, an illustration at best serves to portray a distinct view of the world. We count on the text to establish the credibility

of their claims.

It's the difference in saying "we are all better than everyone else" and "we want you to consider our collective point of view." By adjusting the tone of the conversation, we invite the reader to decide, which is a more believable approach.

I decided to explore a series of objects this great bunch of guys could show up in,

objects whose functions would be affected by their presence.

I chose the sketch of the archer because it was the most dynamic one. There is a sense of tension in its composition, but the strength in the drawing is its surprise. It is a picture we probably have seen before, but reconsider once we notice the three figured arrows.

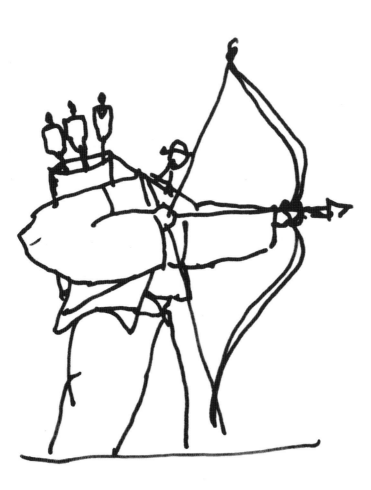
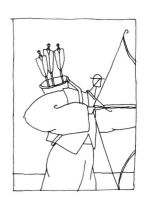
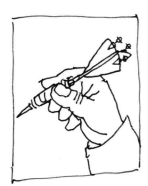
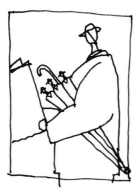
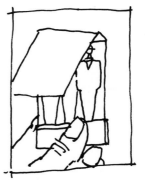

The mind's library. A cover for the book section of the *Boston Globe*, the section featured a book that cited the year's top short stories.

I wanted to illustrate the fact that this was a book about books. I used a technique where I fill a silhouette with another scene. This was handy because of the redundancy of the message.

I started by filling the book with a library of books. I liked the seated figure, but the point of view was too straight on and distant. In order to move the viewer's point of view, I had to sacrifice the library in the book. It was luck that I used the silhouette of his head to relocate the library—in that it is probably where the author would like his work to rest.

In the refinement of the idea, I looked, as I often do, for subtleties that would improve the design of the drawing. I went back to the club chair and reflected the spiral line in the back with the line in his sleeve. I must have felt that the lines on the page fought with the books in his head, so I edited them out.

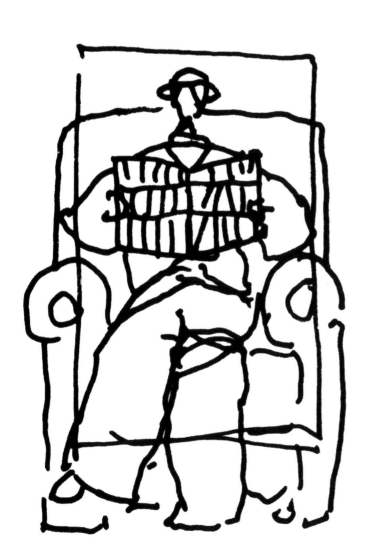

79

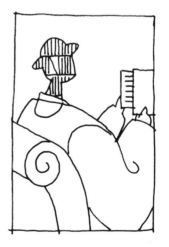

3

Work. The nature of it.

As much as we'd like to be in complete charge of our careers, we're not. Our work is, to a great extent, steered by those who hire us. That's not to say that we shouldn't handpick the kinds of work we accept and set the bar high. But the fact remains that assignments come in all forms, and we would do well to exploit their diversity to the benefit of our own progress.

A number of elements make up the DNA of an assignment. Graphic designers are different from advertising art directors, who are different from magazine art directors. And each one goes about their business as distinctively as the other. Add to the project a client, a budget, a writer, an audience, a deadline, and you have a recipe for an array of results—not all equally satisfying. This is the very nature of our work.

We try to size up each job and dovetail it with our own work discipline. With practice, we learn to read the signals and jump on and off the train more gracefully than the time before.

Every project comes with its own redeeming features. While one may attract us because we feel a kinship with the message, another may showcase our work to a million viewers. And another may pay us generously. Together, they all comprise a breadth of experience that shapes the personal voice of our work.

Pondering. "Managing oneself" was the title of this article for *Harvard Business Review*. A piece about high achievers and how they improve their performance. Like many articles for this publication, this was an examination of human behavior and how it is affected by modern business.

Though the piece described several suggestions on how to improve one's effectiveness, its premise was rooted in the need for self-awareness. Understand first, change second.

Attempting to illustrate the idea of "coming to terms" with oneself, I cast the figure in a literal moment of personal reflection. The symmetrical quality of the drawing established a peaceful setting that was a perfect contrast to the imperfect reflection in the water, a subtle expression of the difficulty in seeing ourselves clearly.

Editorial. A short shelf-life. I never set out to be an editorial illustrator, but for some reason I always have at least one magazine or newspaper assignment on the board at all times. The only thing better would be to have two or three, and the only thing worse would be to have ten. It's a special breed of work, and illustrators tend to thrive on a moderate diet of it.

Editorial work is the perfect training ground for advertising and design jobs. It is quick, topical, interesting, and posts your work every thirty days for the public's critique. The money's not always great, but the deposits to the confidence bank can be huge.

Magazine art directors have a lot to teach about hiring illustrators. The really good ones have such a big-picture view of their magazines they don't have time to tell you what to draw. In fact, they don't want to. What they want is something you have never done before and no other magazine has shown before.

Illustrators are one of the secret weapons in the newsstand wars. And because the war never ends, art directors want relationships with their illustrators. If the first job goes alright, they will be calling again, sometimes in desperation. A long-term working relationship with an art director and his editorial staff is a gift for both parties.

There is an urgency to editorial work that creates both anxiety and comfort. There is not a lot of time to toil over the assignment, and it will be on the street in no time once it's finished. If I'm really proud of the piece, the month on the newsstand passes as if it were only a few days. If I don't think I did so well, it seems to last forever. Weekly magazines and newspapers are even quicker, and more ephemeral.

Unlike other kinds of work, editorial operates in the here and now, and is relatively devoid of the committees that can worry a good idea off the page. Not that there aren't lousy publications out there, but the best ones operate with a spirit of ambition and an understanding that if we don't get it right this time, we will next issue.

Intellectual challenge. I was lucky to be exposed early to the editorial world through work for *Harvard Business Review*. My first assignment was an article about intellectual property rights, the idea of protecting a company's innovations.

Off to a good start, I developed a rapport with the art

director and eventually his editor. Over several years, I produced feature illustrations on a regular basis.

The subjects for the magazine are never dull or easy to digest. Needless to say, they are not easy to solve either. The key to working on these pieces, or any other for that matter,

is being interested in the subject, the author's point of view, or both.

My tenure with the art director lasted for a couple of years until he eventually moved on. I owe a great deal of my experience and confidence to the opportunities and trust he afforded me.

Information drought. As part of the intellectual property article, this made the point that those who receive more information tend to be more innovative than those who receive less.

Profiting from others. This was an article about the big business of nonprofit companies.

COMPETING IN THE INFORMATION ECONOMY

Squeezing today's innovations into yesterday's system simply won't work.

NEEDED: A NEW SYSTEM OF INTELLECTUAL PROPERTY RIGHTS

BY LESTER C. THUROW

FUNDAMENTAL SHIFTS IN TECHNOLOGY and in the economic landscape are rapidly making the current system of intellectual property rights unworkable and ineffective. Designed more than 100 years ago to meet the simpler needs of an industrial era, it is an undifferentiated, one-size-fits-all system. Although treating all advances in knowledge in the same way may have worked when most patents were granted for new mechanical devices, today's brainpower industries pose challenges that are far more complex.

Consider the case of the physician who noticed a relationship between an elevated level of a particular human hormone and a congenital birth defect. He was awarded a patent for his observation,

Lester C. Thurow is the Jerome and Dorothy Lemelson Professor of Management and Economics at the Massachusetts Institute of Technology's Sloan School of Management in Cambridge.

ARTWORK BY CRAIG FRAZIER   HARVARD BUSINESS REVIEW   September–October 1997   94   95

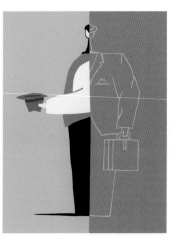

The road to the top. This illustration described the choices we all come up against in regards to our home and work life. It was an easy article with which to identify, and thus easy to portray. I drew a simple metaphor with no right answer.

Rocket science. Here, I illustrated an article about the mechanism of organizations and how results are actually created. The lesson to learn: keep moving.

Feeling like a leader. What makes a leader? According to this article, it's all about emotional intelligence. The great leaders have a full spectrum of development upstairs.

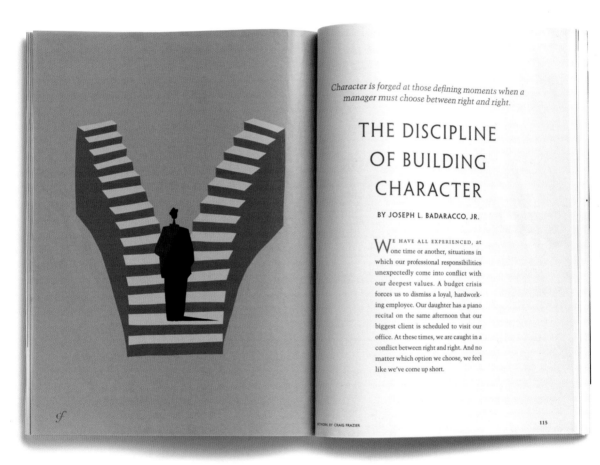

Character is forged at those defining moments when a manager must choose between right and right.

THE DISCIPLINE OF BUILDING CHARACTER

BY JOSEPH L. BADARACCO, JR.

W E HAVE ALL EXPERIENCED, at one time or another, situations in which our professional responsibilities unexpectedly come into conflict with our deepest values. A budget crisis forces us to dismiss a loyal, hardworking employee. Our daughter has a piano recital on the same afternoon that our biggest client is scheduled to visit our office. At these times, we are caught in a conflict between right and right. And no matter which option we choose, we feel like we've come up short.

ARTWORK BY CRAIG FRAZIER   115

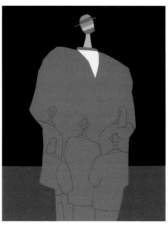

Two-dollar lesson. There are illustrations that, over time, stand out in my mind for one reason or another. This is one of them. It was a personal breakthrough on a couple of different levels.

The first was in terms of the attitude of the illustration. This *Harvard Business Review* article was about executives' view of pay—the fact that most of them believed in out-of-date myths and were generally misinformed on the subject. The article was direct and critical.

I presented a drawing that I felt reflected the author's frank and cynical sentiment. I found the style of writing honest and easy to respond to.

The figure stands with arms crossed, looking straight ahead, his view shrouded by two dollar bills tied to his head. He seems focused and fixed in his posture—unaware of his periphery.

The second breakthrough was in the drawing itself. Since I am always trying to be as simple and graphic as possible, I wrestle with the amount of detail a drawing will have. Up to this point, I had been confining myself to very flat silhouettes that tended to be drawn either head-on or in profile.

In this case, I needed to draw him in more of a three-quarter view in order to better describe his crossed arms and reveal the second dollar bill. I realized that if I could incorporate the slightest bit of line work, I could add a lot more information and interest.

I was inspired by Picasso's drawings of seated men—how his line so fluidly described the folds in their clothes' fabric.

I worked from one of my early sketches and tried to maintain its gesture and style, while keeping it simple. Every element had to be drawn with no greater detail than the next. I edited the design of the dollar bill to its bare essentials—too much information would be distracting. By making the lines in his coat dark gray, the boldness of the overall figure is not sacrificed. The string is red to bring just the right amount of attention to it. His hands are as minimal as possible. Two ivory triangles define the openings in his one-button coat.

I look at this illustration frequently to remind me of its recipe: appropriate doses of idea, attitude, and execution.

Group effort. A series of full-pagers for a special section in *Business Week*. The assignment asked for simple, iconic descriptions of several industry sectors to be used as section openers. Because these were divider pages and had to allow consistent typography, central figures on bold backgrounds were just the answer. It is always a fun exercise creating these graphic associations between characters and their activities. I like the simple melding of idea and execution.

Each of the topics was so general the possibilities were wide open. I showed many of the sketches to the art director and we agreed on most of our choices, based on how well they worked as a group.

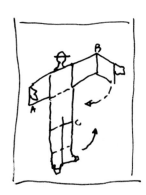

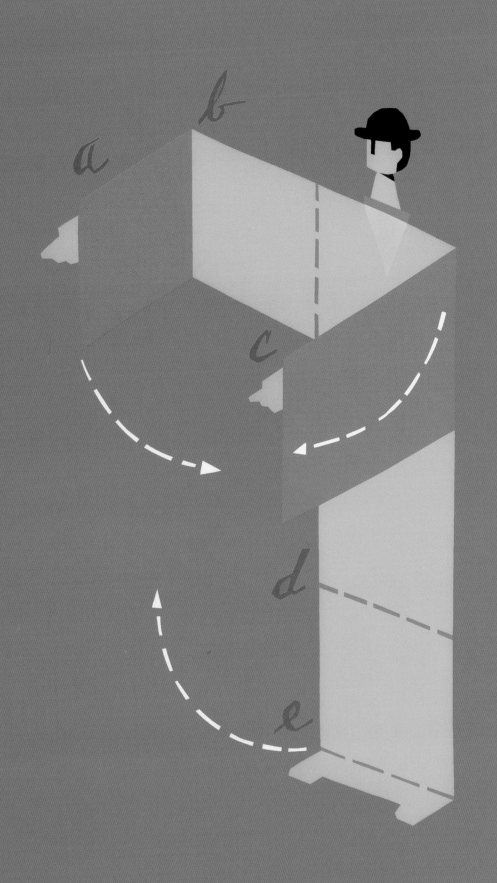

90

Mending Italy. This was an illustration describing Italy's ailing political situation for the international issue of *Business Week*. I couldn't resist the urge to use the classic icon of the Italian boot. I felt so strongly about the idea, I only presented the art director two options — sitting or standing! We both agreed that the standing position probably depicted our subject as more positive and on the mend. The boot also looked more like the position on the map we tend to remember.

© 2002 Dow Jones & Company, Inc. All Rights Reserved.

MONDAY, FEBRUARY 11, 2002

THE WALL STREET JOURNAL   **R1**

E-COMMERCE

THE HARD CASES

Why some industries have been failures on the Net –
and how they may find success after all

by Michael Totty and Ann Grimes

PAGE 6

ALSO IN THIS ISSUE

SHOPPING ADDICT
OR ENTHUSIAST?
*Shelly Branch tries
to figure out which
she is.* **PAGE 8**

WHAT'S NEXT?
*Lee Gomes takes
a trip to the future
of computing.* **PAGE 9**

FIXING
THE FLAWS
*Scott Thurm on how
Internet2 hasn't done
all it was supposed to.*
PAGE 13

IT'S IN THE DELIVERY
*The solution to e-commerce
may be a box. Pui-Wing Tam
explains how.* **PAGE 14**

MAKE ME LAUGH
*Alex Frangos asks humorists
what's so funny on the Web.* **PAGE 17**

frazier

Concept shopping. Sometimes I rush in too soon and overlook the obvious. I struggled for quite some time with this section opener for the *Wall Street Journal*. It talked about retail companies that had failed to sell with any great success on the Internet.

The problem I encountered was that I focused too much on the idea of retail on the Internet, and not enough on the failure aspect. Although the sketch of the landscape of laptops hinted at it, it didn't make the point very clearly.

After rejecting my initial ideas, the art director and I were able to better identify the theme. Because e-commerce was stated in the header,

I realized that I didn't need to explain it again visually.

So I abandoned the Internet angle and pursued the idea of a broken retail situation, thus, the shopping cart and its flat tires. Everyone loved it and I was given a green light.

My favorite part of the drawing is the Mickey Mouse–style tires with shiny white highlights.

PUMPING TIRE UP.

Civic duty. The OpEd section of the *New York Times* is the fifty-yard dash of illustrator's assignments. With usually twenty-four hours between start and finish, these assignments offer little in the way of time to reflect or reconsider. Beyond that, they usually express important opinions about weighty topics that will appear in the most widely read newspaper in the world!

I rarely turn these assignments down unless I strongly disagree with the author's opinion or I need a full night's sleep. I consider them a privilege and a responsibility.

This was an essay by President Clinton during his last week in office. Though it wasn't what I would have expected to be his last words, I'm sure he had his reasons. In essence, he commented on America's

progress, or lack thereof, in eliminating racial borders.

I went to work looking at relationships with the flag, which I quickly abandoned because they were overstating the American part of the story. The art director approved the sketch of the two figures studying their conflicting shadows across the same line. Late that night, I made an executive decision to include a third figure

and change the line to an X. It now became a more diverse group, with the X representing the convergence of multiple lines and a central focus of attention. It became a more interesting illustration. I made the lines dotted to allude to the fact that they are fading, but far from gone.

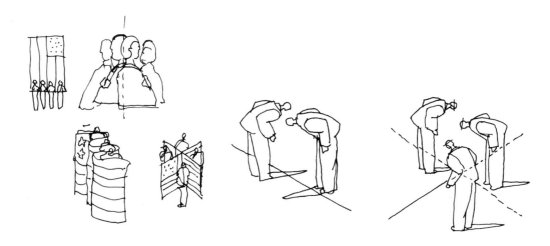

The mighty pen. These assignments are always quick and always easy to misinterpret. I don't know which is worse: the fear of missing the deadline, or making it and looking like an idiot to a million people.

This particular piece was an essay about the Antiballistic Missile Treaty and President Bush's right to negate it. The argument made was that if it required two-thirds of the Senate vote to enter the original treaty, then it should take the same to do away with it. This point was only being argued because the Bush camp felt he could accomplish it alone, which brought into play the question whether it was the right decision at all.

Needless to say, I wrestled with the point of the article before I wrestled with the symbols I was going to use. As is often the case, these articles aren't necessarily easy to visually summarize, especially in less than a day.

My initial sketch was rejected by the editor. The art director and I argued that the pen was a proper symbol for the treaty signing, and by making it a fulcrum, the direction it would tip would be determined by the will of people at either end—not just the holder of the pen.

Our argument won over the editor's opinion—two to one.

95

Watchful eye. A cover about our exposure on the Internet and who's watching us. By using the curtain as a symbol for privacy, I was able to introduce the element of an intruder. The figure's crossed arms, outstretched fingers and leery eye indicate his concern for his identity.

Summer reading. A whimsical drawing for a review of summer fiction. An early piece using the unlikely transposition of a book for a saddle. On a big, black stallion under a golden sky, the character rides through a seemingly fictional summer scene.

Faceless. This was a cover story about the 2004 presidential hopeful Howard Dean. Though he is the nation's longest serving Democratic governor, he is completely unknown to the national press and the country at large. It was a favorable article about a man with virtually no public identity—so far.

On Time. This was one of my first newsstand covers—an article naming the nation's top leaders under forty. I started with the trusty torch as a symbol for leadership, then incorporated a face in the flame to suggest the leader's identity. A simple twist, but without it this illustration would never have made the cover.

Covers. Judging the book. There is nothing quite like having your work on the cover of a newsstand magazine. There is the sense that you are taking part in the constantly changing visual journal of our culture. Though that may be a romanticized picture, there is no getting around a magazine cover's inherent power to signify the times to the passerby. And even though a great deal of its influence lies in the hands of the art director and the reputation of the magazine, we take a cover assignment as if it was our final project.

The ideas and thinking required by a cover are, for the most part, no different from any other editorial assignment. However, the elements of design, typography, and the need for instant readability, combined with our own strict criteria, make illustrating covers into projects of seemingly grand proportion.

But face it, the real job of the cover is to sell magazines. Nothing broadcasts what's on the inside better than what's on the outside. Magazines are judged by their covers. Accepting this fact doesn't change our role or suddenly make the job more commercial, but it explains the context, which makes it unlike any other kind of assignment.

The seasoned art director knows that left alone, a good illustrator will pour more than is needed into the project and will likely deliver in spades. Just as a cover has to sell the magazine to its readers—it has to sell the illustrator to his clients. It is the codependent nature of this relationship that keeps us both honest and contributing heartily to each other's benefit.

WHAT KIND OF WAR? LAWRENCE F. KAPLAN, MICHELLE COTTLE, JEFFREY ROSEN, MARTIN PERETZ, YOSSI KLEIN HALEVI, RYAN LIZZA, LEON WIESELTIER, PETER BEINART, THE EDITORS

THE **NEW REPUBLIC**

OCTOBER 15, 2001

SPECIAL
Fall Books Issue

HOW NOT
TO WRITE
A NOVEL
ABOUT
AMERICA
By James Wood

Plus: Gordon S. Wood
Paula Fredriksen
Ruth Franklin
Fintan O'Toole

$3.50US $3.50CAN
42>

01742
0 787446 8

Hard at it. Sometimes an assignment calls up a picture that has been waiting in the back of my mind for a home. This was one of those cases.

When I think about a novel writer, I have this image of him hunched over an old Smith-Corona, pecking on the keys, with pages of fiction spewing out prolifically.

This cover was about the American novel and the difficulty involved in trying to write one. It was a cynical discussion referring to the recent works of one author, about the fact that the great American novel is quickly dated by the very culture it attempts to describe. It portrayed the author's job as tiresome and futile.

Nonetheless, it was still about the writer I had seen earlier in my mind. All I had to do was make it work on the page and include an American reference somewhere.

I was most interested in the attitude and composition of the illustration. Sympathetic to the writer, I cast him hard at work, lip jutting out and determined to write an American classic.

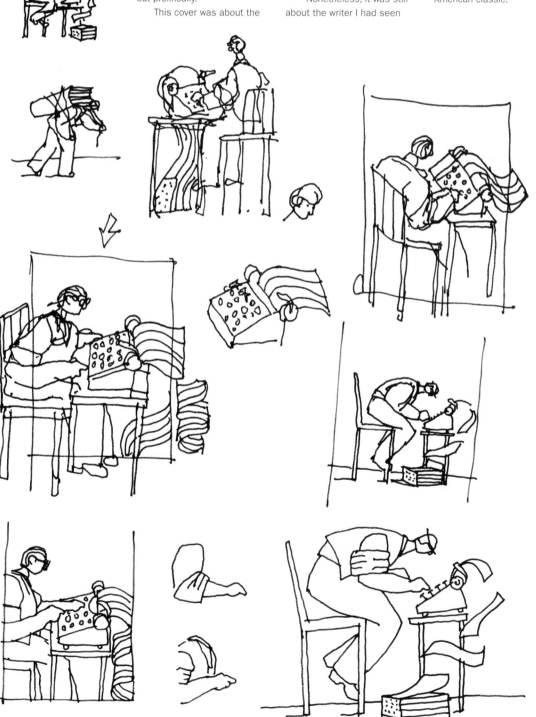

Private eyes. Privacy on the Internet is a growing concern. I had illustrated a similar subject earlier for the *Utne Reader,* (page 84), but took a slightly different approach this time.

Invasion of privacy creates a creepy sense of being secretly watched by someone. It's an emotional violation of our space. I explored several symbols and scenarios attempting to describe it with the right tone. Pleased with a few of them, I did quick color studies and showed them to the art director for his choice. I don't usually do this, but was in a quandary myself choosing the right one. He picked the keyhole and said it ultimately worked best with the typography, and was also probably the boldest.

This cover has quite a different feeling from the other possibilities. We are observers in the others, whereas we are participants in this one. The over-scaled keyhole begs the question, "are we invading his privacy," or "is this shifty-looking guy invading ours?"

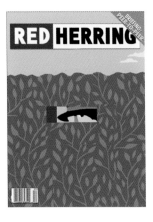
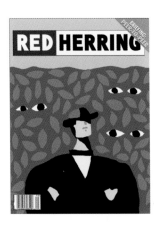

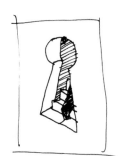

Work. Covers.

OPEN LETTER TO THE PRESIDENT

RED HERRING

THE BUSINESS OF TECHNOLOGY

DIVX;-)
Can a hacker
technology go legit? **PAGE 60**

TELCOS
Debt, cheap bandwidth,
and other bad news **PAGE 66**

VCs POST CRASH
Life after the party **PAGE 32**

101

Privacy

Why it
will shape
e-commerce
in 2001

PAGE 48

Series. Working thematically. I love big projects, assignments with lots of illustrations, series of illustrations speaking with the same voice. An opportunity to tell, within a designed setting, a number of small stories, each staking out the corners of a central theme. Each one is created with a courteous relationship both to the previous one and the one to follow, neither stealing the other's thunder, collectively composing a tapestry of expression made from a common thread.

Quite the opposite of a *New York Times* assignment, creating series are more of an illustrator's marathon than a sprint. They require thinking in a more linear fashion, taking into account pacing, sequencing, and continuity. They are more like movies than snapshots. They are more like sentences than words.

While working on a series tends to take the pressure off creating the single quintessential illustration, it imposes a different pressure to create a full cast of winners. Every idea has to be formulated knowing there is a bigger story to tell—and that a weak link detracts from the strength of the whole. It's more than a group of drawings with similar colors and elements, they are sides to the same cube, upholding each other to create a form of greater dimension.

Series are the lifeblood of successful advertising campaigns, annual reports, and corporate branding programs. Working in series is not only economical but resoundingly effective. It is a place where an illustrator can noticeably contribute to the creation and expressiveness of a company's voice.

Celestial currency. Sometimes the surprise of an unfamiliar setting lends enough novelty to initiate the conversation.

Like so many businesses, describing a bank goes beyond its day-to-day operation. It becomes much more about features like size, relationships, and customer service.

Netbank wanted its annual report to describe several of those features of its business.

One of the directions I explored made an obvious reference to banking by using dramatically oversized coins throughout. Another alternative was a series using the night sky as the stage. The client preferred this direction.

Having no direct connection to their industry, I think it created a more philosophical tone than the expected vernacular of the financial world.

Commonplace messages like "profitable partnerships" suddenly assumed new meaning when they were described using new symbols. Substituting stars for currency brought a sense of wonderment and appreciation for the job of working together to make a profit.

103

It takes two. The Fremont Group produced an annual report devoted specifically to the theme of partners. Not a new theme for an illustration, but new for a series of six illustrations. I decided right away that there would have to be some degree of illusion or visual contradiction taking place in each illustration to make the theme go the distance. With thanks to M.C. Escher, this was some of the most fun I've had doing an annual report. I wish I could remember the secret of creating the illusions. All I can say is that it is a function of sketching lots of scenarios and playing with the optics of each one until something magical happens.

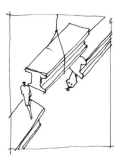
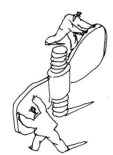

104

Home, sweet home. Buying a home is a nervous proposition. Traditional real estate companies have a reputation for touting mortgage rates and sales records as a way to get in the door. They're not always empathetic to the new buyer.

This was a series of illustrations for a new real estate

company attempting to make a name for itself. They were used in ads, billboards, brochures, and bus sides. The campaign's messaging centered on building the credibility of the fledgling company, rather than the individual agent's.

With the tagline, "There's no place like home," it was a

chance to make illustrations that were friendly, humorous, and fun—to create a brand that spoke with a warm and charming voice.

107

Royal family. I was asked to create a family of illustrations as identities for twelve grades in the Wausau Paper line. They appeared on swatchbooks, posters, and promotional materials. The papers had been named years ago, and most carried the adjective "royal" in their name, such as Royal Silk and Royal Laid. Wausau had never taken advantage of this cue for the papers' visuals, but it seemed a natural direction for exploiting the connection.

The assignment was twelve cover illustrations and about fifteen related spots. It turned into an exploration of billowy costumes, regal figures, and visual puns. I worked on them for about eight months, with two or three in progress at all times.

This was a jewel of an assignment to work on. Because the audience was designers, I felt that the illustrations should be bright and whimsical.

I did quite a bit of research on costumes, though I didn't bind them to any particular period or style. I'm sure I made some gross errors in dress and adornment that would cause social disgrace to some of the subjects. In the meantime, I got a lot better at drawing armor and pleated collars.

WAUSAU ROYAL SILK

Selling linen. In illustrating Royal Linen, I showed a couple of different scenarios. A dining king and a reclining queen—both humorous depictions of linen. The king was perhaps the more prudent choice.

Just white. For Royal Bright White I couldn't resist drawing the lily-white stallion. Not nearly as clever as some of the other illustrations, this one is more an exercise in extremes. The dark sky, colorful armor and plumes all contrast dramatically with the starkness of the white horse.

Charming prince. I saw two ways to illustrate this one. The paper, Royal Laid, could be identified either by referencing the paper's surface or by a very silly play on words.

In imitating the paper's woven surface, I drew a dashing prince standing in front of an iron trellis. In hindsight, the subtle description of the "laid weave" in his clothing and the trellis may be a bit abstract to get immediately.

I think the "egg laying" cover might have been a little too cute but it had a lot of other redeeming features. The goose was charming and the collar was going to be very whimsical and graphic. Of course, his coat also mimicked the laid pattern of the paper. I like his classic posture, seemingly unaware of his additional adornment.

In any case, the prince got the job and the king didn't.

111

Raw trust. I have been eating at a particular sushi bar for twenty years. When he was expanding, the owner asked me if I would design a new menu for him. Since I had been waiting for some time for this request, I couldn't resist the temptation to do more. By the time the expansion was complete I had redesigned his logo,

signage, menus, chopstick holders, and created a series of illustrations that adorned the walls and wine bottles.

The restaurant is a contemporary Japanese sushi bar with great regard for its new and loyal customers. The illustrations and design were a result of knowing the owner, his business and personal style quite

well. His respect and trust in my work was rewarding.

The series of illustrations posed very stylized silhouettes entwined in delicate seaweed with magic fish passing through the scene. Each was complemented with an icon of Japanese cuisine. A graphic fantasy world, perhaps a nod to a patron's dining experience.

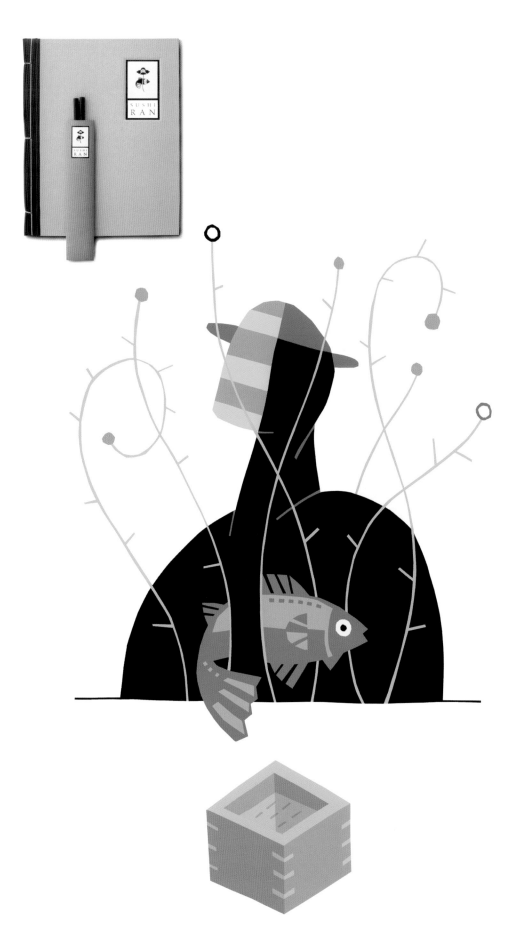

113

Moving ahead. Following the stock market's severe decline in 2002, financial companies began to gear their communications toward retaining and regaining their credibility in the minds of an increasingly skeptical audience. Companies' messaging started to talk about notions like "preparedness for a turnaround" and "slow and steady" returns on investments, contrary to the high-growth promises of the recent past.

Such was the case on the annual report for a mutual fund group where the theme was "momentum." The report's messaging centered around the company's break from its former holding company and fresh start with a seasoned, proven team—creating an organization with diverse subsidiaries and a strong urge to build a progressive new brand.

With topics like "a diversity of specialties, all pulling in the same direction," and "positioning for recovery," I proposed a series of drawings that cast small figures as integral elements in large mechanisms, each mechanism illustrating a principle described in the accompanying text. I felt that the repeated use of multiple figures served to represent the company's expert subsidiaries in the context of achieving a collective result.

I kept the illustrations to a palette of four colors and several shades of gray. I drew androgynous figures and used line and texture to create volume and detail. I established a low point-of-view to create the most dramatic composition of each machine and operator. I tried to make each illustration as if it was a freeze frame in a moving picture—with a credible sense of power and elegance.

114

4

Voice. The style of speaking.

As our illustrated voice grows clearer and more conversant, so does our interest in contributing to a heightened level of conversation. We lean toward, and attract, work that consciously or unconsciously improves our skills at telling a story. We develop a greater range of expression. We reach a more evolved understanding of our various audiences and the dialects necessary to effectively speak to them. And we develop methods that we revisit and learn to trust. We develop the style of our own voice.

Once aware of that style, the real work begins. Our task reaches beneath the surface of our drawings and into the unconscious tone of their expressions. We look for ways in which to modulate their volume, pitch, and rhythm. The search for "a more elegant way to say it" is forever ongoing. But it is exactly this pursuit that gives our work continuity over time, and defines the highly personal nature of the job. There is no road map for this journey, it is simply a product of time and a diligent hunger to reach an intuitive stride.

Our job requires a healthy discontent for the things that flow easily from our fingers, while at the same time accepting that they define the very style that is unavoidably our own.

Fully integrated. The message here was how to manage growth by managing technology. In many ways this was made easier by suggesting the connection between two very different notions. Growth is always easier to visualize than technology. In this case, I created a relationship that served to symbolize both. The vines and hedge obviously represent growth, but they also represent technology in the aspects of networks and integration. I implied a further union of the two by connecting the hedge and the observer. What was once an obstruction is now part of him and may even contribute to his ability to see beyond.

118

Metaphors. In other words.

The difference in representational and conceptual illustration is defined as much by their distinct appearances as their distinct purposes. Representational illustration is bound by the reality of what it attempts to portray. Its degree of interpretation is controlled by the context and accuracy of its rendition. Its goal is to bring a heightened aesthetic to something familiar to us. Conceptual illustration, on the other hand, strays from reality and attempts to express, through a combination of real and unreal representations, a scenario that requires interpretation. Its goal, to tell a story that asks the viewer to connect the dots and take part in fashioning its message.

It has always been my interest as a designer and illustrator to work conceptually. This is not to say there isn't due call for representational illustration and design, it just hasn't been what flows from my pen. That said, it would be impossible to work conceptually without a good sense of how to draw things with a fair degree of resemblance to reality.

The visual metaphor is by far my most practiced and trusted approach to illustration. I began working with metaphors early on while designing trademarks, and still believe they are the best way to provoke a viewer's participation.

Metaphors are the perfect vehicle for explaining the abstract. They spark curiosity and fascination in the otherwise mundane. They defamiliarize the commonplace. They personify a single point of view. They are road signs that tickle our imaginations and grant us permission to think in new terms.

I enjoy creating metaphors as much as I do looking at them. To be successful, they require a certain sequence of suppositions that collectively compose a theory, and in context conjure an event in the viewer's mind. A delicate if/then proposition that needs to transmit at lightning speed with little room for miscues. From a creator's perspective, the sheer number of variables involved make for a picture game where it's easier to miss than it is to hit. Nonetheless, practice is the only antidote for the nervous illustrator in search of "other words."

THE WALL STREET JOURNAL REPORTS.

© 2001 Dow Jones & Company, Inc. All Rights Reserved.

THE WALL STREET JOURNAL **R1**

TAX PLANNING

NEW LAWS, NEW STRATEGIES

For many people, tax planning means simply keeping their current tax bills as low as possible. With this year's historic tax package, now is the time to start thinking more broadly.

IT ISN'T TOO LATE
Tom Herman offers
some last-minute
tax tips
R4

THE NEW COLLEGE TRY
Aaron Lucchetti
tells why paying for
an education just got
a little easier
R4

WINNING THE BATTLE, LOSING THE WAR
Kortney Stringer
reveals the pitfalls of
tax-managed mutual funds
R6

HEIR TODAY...
Paralyzed by
estate-tax confusion?
Lynn Asinof explains why
that's a big mistake.
R8

Staying sharp. I am fascinated by the simplest objects and mechanisms and love it when I can find a place for them in my work. I am also intrigued by the possibility of altering our view just enough to cause us to think twice about our routine realities. Call it surrealism or just graphic high jinks, I'm attracted to this approach.

On this assignment, my job was to create an illustration that signaled that there was some new thinking about the old ways to go about accounting and taxes. I presented two sketches and the art director used both, for the cover and the inside.

Recalling the adage of "sharpening your pencil" for accuracy, the pencil sharpener made a good symbol to start with. It's a primitive cause-and-effect device that lends itself to altering the expected outcome. On first glance, we think we see a pencil shaving coming out as it's supposed to, then we realize that the entire pencil is emerging as if pressed out from under a rolling pin. I added a curious miniature onlooker just to further obscure the reality, a whimsical view of a not-so-whimsical subject.

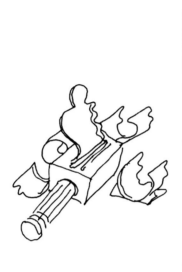 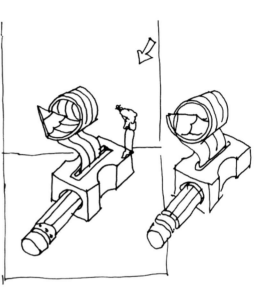

121

Within reach. This was an opener for an article discussing current college graduates' affinity for business degrees. I illustrated the idea of being lured by something inherently desirable. Beyond the expected meaning of the dangling carrot, I felt that this piece needed to convey a sense that it would be intrinsically good for him, hence the carrot-like vest. This was something he had tasted before. The article points out that though the degree is generally attractive, thoughtful consideration about how attainable and realistic it is in today's business world is critical. So I drew the figure sitting in the chair looking pensive about the prospect ahead.

I tied the stick on his head to imply a sense that he was "strapped" with this situation— perhaps of his own doing.

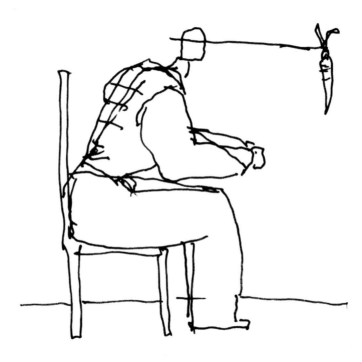

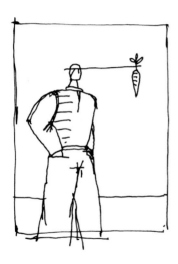 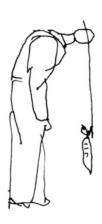 

Tall order. There is something about a book cover that seems to bring about greater consideration than other assignments. Maybe it's the public permanence or the worry that the book might be judged by my work alone.

I think the irony of this book title touched off my curiosity.

"Excuse me, your life is waiting." I read the manuscript and maintained my original hunch that the cover should be as whimsical as the title. As well-meaning and purposeful as the content was, its aspirational nature signaled a lighthearted metaphor for the cover.

Assuming a reader finds

himself in the market for a book like this, it seemed appropriate that the illustration portray a reasonable amount of risk with a high degree of personal return. Like saying, "Come on in, the water's fine—as long as you like water."

125

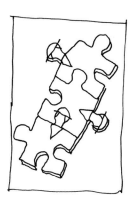
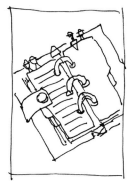
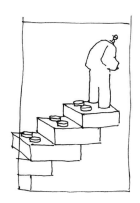

126

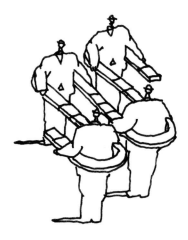

High expectations. As a page in a sales manual for 3Com Corporation, this illustration portrays the company's tall expectations for their sales staff (book shown on page 66).

The company deals in network systems and their clients rely on them. The message served to identify their sales prospects and their essential characteristics. In essence, they were described as driven to success and highly dependent on the networks their businesses were built on.

The book took a no-frills tone in its approach. A failed network was severely consequential for a business.

Because the specifics of technology can be tough to explain, I look for elementary symbols to help. Toys can be amazing and very symbolic upon close inspection. Legos are a notable graphic form and resemble large, plastic pixels. They were well-suited for this metaphor, strong and predictable, yet vulnerable to gravity and poor assembly.

Stacked up and going in a positive direction, these blocks told the story. I made the figure integral to the assembly to accentuate his dependence. He's confidently looking upward, trusting the system beneath his feet. He's in the exact place he wants to be.

Schools of thought. This article was for a design magazine discussing the future of navigation on the Internet. I was initially concerned about the technical nature of the article, and that it might be limiting, but decided that I could do something fun for the magazine's audience of designers.

Leaving the details of the technological forecasting to the text, I decided to explore the thought that directional signals don't always appear in the same places or the same form, the idea that the direction of directions is changing.

I eventually settled on the idea of a guy looking deep into the water with a flashlight. Our submarine view reveals that he illuminates two schools of fish pointing in opposite directions.

This served to point out two things: first that directions can be found in the least obvious places; and second, that they may still require decoding.

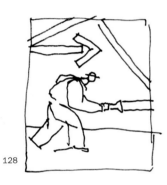   

Flip-flopped. It looked like a pretty easy assignment from the project brief, a cover for a special travel section for a national Sunday paper. In fact, I thought it was a chance to do something new. No specific places, no particular means of travel, no sponsors to please. No agenda. Looked like fun.

I proposed this illustration with great enthusiasm. It reminded me of a classic travel poster. It was graphic, humorous, and presented a romantic view of travel.

The client didn't see it that way and rejected the sketch. So I finished an alternative sketch and this one as well, in hopes that they would change their mind. Regrettably, they didn't.

Misfires. Picking up the pieces. **Failed attempts are an inevitable reality of the illustrator's job. Call them the fallout of miscommunication, an overly literal client, an unbridled committee, or our own lack of the right stuff. Failures can crop up at any time, for any number of reasons. Regardless of the specific rationale, they tend to be an unwelcome bump in the road—at least at the time. Though labeling them failures connotes a dreadful outcome, they rarely measure up to more than an errant shot at a steadily moving target. And in short time they vanish into the shadows of experience.**

I usually show a client a couple of ideas unless the assignment is a quick editorial piece. The client's selection of one sketch is always at the expense of the other. In effect, one of the ideas either failed to do the job or the other just succeeded a little better. I have found that nothing guards against failure like numbers. A client's exposure to alternative solutions for the same problem tends to invite enthusiastically favorable responses.

A rejected idea doesn't necessarily mean the illustration would fail the purpose for which it was intended. Or that our thinking is completely offtrack. It means that the client's expectation has not been met. Ironically, there is nothing quite like a presentation of ideas to bring clarity to a client's expectations. Like it or not, ideas are dismissed for completely subjective reasons as frequently as they are for objective or rational reasons. It is important to recognize the difference, at the time, if we are to positively benefit from the experience.

Whether I stay on an assignment or not, following a rejection, is based on how I read the client's signals. Sometimes it's an easy fix. Sometimes it's clear we are mismatched. In any case, I often complete the illustration. On occasion, the client will be moved to reverse their decision. Usually, however, it amounts to a personal exercise in proving out my hunch to myself—a sort of self-preservation mechanism. I've found that the intrinsic value in finishing an idea far outweighs the alternative of an early dismissal.

Not amused. At first I thought it fit perfectly. What better way to illustrate the idea of a firm providing custom-tailored insurance. Especially if they insure circuses and other amusement shows. This was one time when a clown seemed to be exactly the right messenger for the job.

The client didn't share my witty view, and asked for another take, something more specific to an insurance situation. Reluctantly, I drew an accident on the verge of happening. It worked fine.

Still happy with the clown, I finished the illustration and put him in the portfolio. He was eventually called on to audition for a leading role in a national ad campaign (see following page).

Too much fun. "Work in, play out" was the message of this billboard campaign for Chevrolet. The idea was to illustrate the many uses of the van's new sliding doors.

Originally, they asked that I put a clown in this illustration after having seen my drawing from the previous page. I did several sketches and everything looked fine until the agency asked that the clown be replaced with somebody else. He could be humorous, even silly, but not a clown. So I introduced the beachcomber and finished the illustration.

The campaign immediately ramped up and I produced several sketches along the same humorous lines. I was doing sketches for ads, catalogues, and there was even talk of animated television spots.

No sooner than the first billboard appeared, the entire campaign was abandoned, with never a clear explanation of what precipitated the decision.

It was surely a disappointment, but not a failure. The inherent danger in large national assignments is the scale of the decision-making process. Unfortunately, for every person saying "bring in the clowns," there's someone else saying "no clowning."

134

Magic bucket. There are certain messages that reoccur with regularity in particular business niches. In the financial world, the notion of choices is a common claim made for everything from customer services to investments. The challenge is always to find an original metaphor.

We contend not only with our client's need to see something new, but our own. Our client's idea of new does not necessarily consider our previous exploits of a topic or our saturation level for the mundane. Our craving for something unconventional often looks like a failed attempt in the eyes of our client.

Such was the case with this drawing for a corporate magazine's article on making the right choice amongst an excess of options offered in the banking industry.

Everything looked good for this sketch until the client said okay with the simple addition of a dollar sign on the bucket's handle. They were concerned that the reader wouldn't make the leap. The client was intractable and the signs were clear that they didn't like my brand of storytelling.

Curious about the drawing, I finished it and sent it to them anyway. It didn't get used but apparently set off a wave of discussion within the company about their tone and style of communication.

I sat with the illustration for some time and eventually used it as the opening scene for my first animation (see page 146).

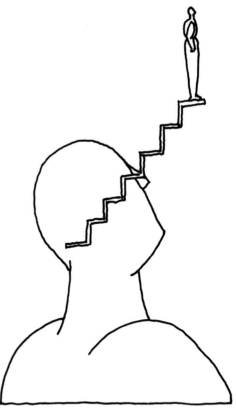

138

Tape critters. I had designed a little two-color, perfect-bound book for a client. Just before going to press, the printer alerted me that we would need a much taller spine than my book had in order to perfect-bind it. Essentially, I had an extra fifty-two-page book running along with this job.

With two days and no concept, I cut twenty-three little critters out of pieces of black tape. The rules: one-and-a-half inch piece of tape, use all the pieces, no sketching, have fun.

My kids were small at the time, and I was inspired by how randomly they made things. Just cut and see what happens.

I mailed out the book to clients and friends and immediately acquired fans for the tiny hand-cut beings. I produced two more books and the collection of critters had grown to sixty-nine. People loved them and I loved making them.

This silly little personal assignment has carried with it long-lasting lessons.

Practice. For the fun of it. There is the work between the work. The things we do to stay sharp. To stay interested. To stay in the game. Call it practice or call it diversion. It's critical to our survival.

We put our hands into self-imposed assignments whose influence and relief creeps its way back into our day jobs. Out of fantasy or naive ambition, we conjure up chores to test our mettle; sometimes, with deliberate purpose complete with deadlines, goals, and rewards; other times with no guidelines, no end in sight, and no indication of payback. And that's okay with us.

The common thread in these assignments is the lure of free rein. No client, no deadline, no criteria. It is the essential ingredient that draws us in and leaves us to fight it out with no one but ourselves. We are left with assignments rife with false expectations, ruthless criticism, and very little encouragement. But we know these assignments are essential for our preservation and our growth.

I have found the greatest value resides in projects that are fun to do. That doesn't mean that they aren't hard or don't present moments of doubt and purpose-lessness. But if I'm enjoying the exercise at the time, even somewhat mindlessly, it's probably going to contribute long after the moment.

Hindsight has revealed that side projects with no specific agendas have always proved the most fruitful. The mere act of working without traditional expectations confuses our own methods and rote processes. We switch to an improvisational mode. We care less. We care more. Our responses in their best moments are raw, intuitive, and surprisingly new, even to us. They are important blips on the screen.

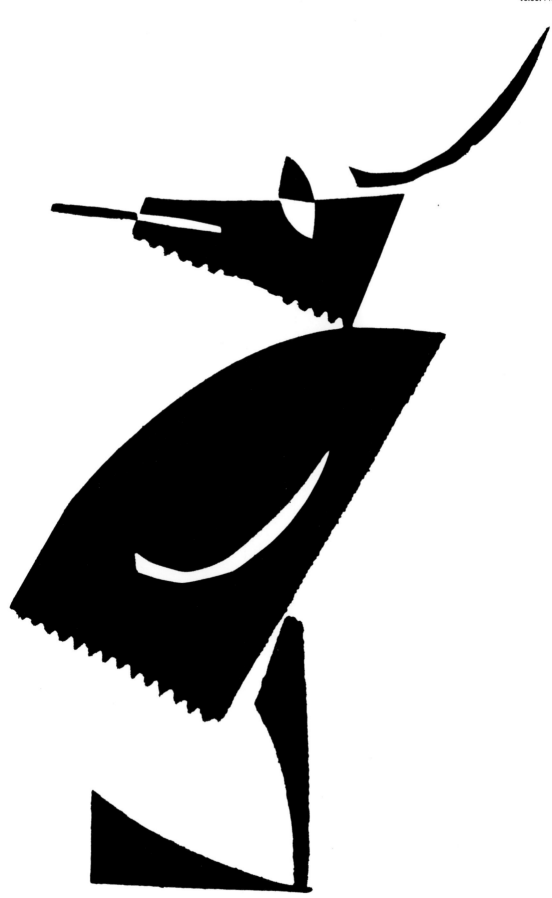

142

143

Bedtime story. At the time of this book's publishing, my second kid's book is nearly completed. It's pretty simple. There are at least ten good reasons not to go to bed. With a house full of animals, there is a good excuse around nearly every corner.

I created a series of two-color drawings of friendly animals in unlikely household settings. I wrote and designed the book as well.

144

I want to turn off my game but there is a mouse on my computer!

I want to read a bedtime story but there is a frog in my chair!

I want to put on my slippers but there is a duck in my closet!

I want to take my bath but there is an elephant in the bathtub!

145

I want to go to sleep but there is a monkey, a duck, a snake, an alligator, an elephant, a koala, a turtle, a mouse, and a frog in my bed!

Keep moving. "What if my illustrations moved? What would they look like?" Every illustrator asks himself this question at some point in time.

Intent on answering the question, I designed my first animation and didn't stop until I had produced five of them.

My first attempt was a graphic little movie that stars Harold, who first appeared in a rejected illustration a year or so previously (page 136). Inspired by *Yellow Submarine,* and the children's animations of Leo Lionni, I set him in motion.

The piece is about eighty seconds long. Harold curiously walks through a world that continuously changes before his eyes. It is a surreal discovery of puddles that morph into holes, into steps, and back into puddles.

I worked with Ian Kovalick and Matt Horn of hillmancurtis, inc. in New York to produce the actual motion and music. Scored with a dreamy audio loop, *Swiss Cheese* was built to play easily on the Internet.

In order to create a viewing home for this movie and the others to follow, I designed the Web site called squarepig.tv. The movies are seen all over the world by kids and adults of numerous cultures.

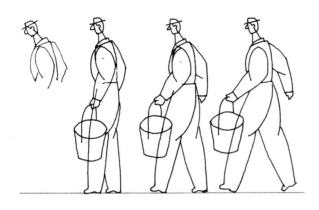

squarepig.tv

146

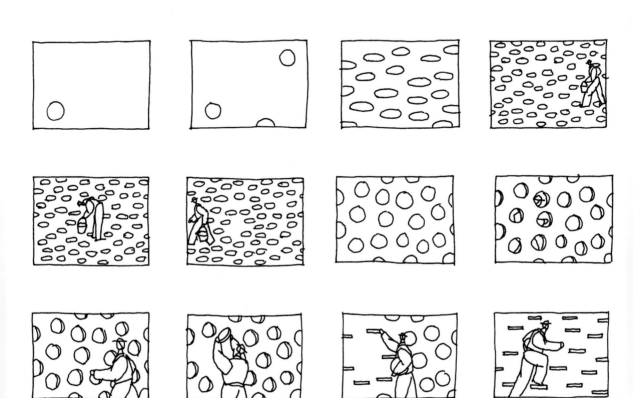

Bladerunning. This movie starred Andrew the gardener and his friend Arnold the garden snake. The two share a lawn—with very different perspectives.

Stymied by the fact that his efforts seem to be undone just as quickly as he completes them, Andrew stops, then shows us his simple and unique problem-solving skills. (You have to see the movie.)

Like *Swiss Cheese*, *Bladerunning* is about eighty seconds long and features a custom soundtrack.

As with all of these movies, they start with a storyboard which I sketch and everyone involved works from; it describes all the moves and transitions. I then draw all of the necessary cells that compose each movement. The production team scores the music and constructs the final piece for Internet viewing.

149

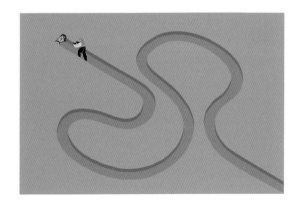

Fire drill. Adobe saw my initial movies and hired me to create a movie for use on the Internet and in their trade show booths. I was to bring a story to their tagline, "Everywhere you look."

I introduced Bart and Arnie, who upon meeting discover fire in Bart's pants. In the course of the ninety-second movie, we learn that this is not like the fire we expect. It isn't harmful, and in fact, is transmitted from one to another through a simple smile and a handshake.

Before you know it, it's everywhere you look.

151

String quartet. The job here was to bring attention to this company's trusted and particularly collaborative partners. They were, by the way, in the mortgage business, not the music business.

Touting a company's people can be a very touchy mission. It serves a legitimate purpose, but handled wrongly, can backfire. An innocent attempt to showcase people can easily look like breast-beating.

In an attempt to avoid that problem, I proposed a way to highlight the partners in an inconspicuous fashion.

By borrowing on the beauty and credibility of the violin, I inserted the figures in place of the tuning pegs. Their association with the instrument, and the job of keeping it in tune, said a lot in a subtle and elegant way.

Tone. Getting through. We all like to be spoken to in a manner that feels both personal and befitting of the moment in time. Given a choice, we usually prefer a gentle and engaging dialogue over a condescending monologue. There are times when a factual presentation is in order, like getting driving directions. And there are times when a whispered three-word phrase of affection speaks volumes. Generally, the tone and pitch of expression has everything to do with the degree to which it is heard.

The tone of voice of illustrations and design is no different. Public symbols tend to be direct and absent of nuance. Cosmetic packaging tends to be allusive and soft-spoken. Children's books tend to be bold and accessible. All designed to prompt very different and desired responses from their particular audiences.

We understand that the content and message of our illustrations vary tremendously according to the nature of the assignment. And over time we learn various dialects that are triggered almost automatically by our read of the problem to be solved. But what is much more elusive and evolving in our bag of tricks is the tone of those expressions. We struggle to color that voice, both literally and figuratively.

Just as in verbal conversation, we can size up a situation and gauge our tone in accordance. In a crowded room or a crowded magazine, sometimes speaking softly at close range is the only answer. Talking across the street requires loud and abbreviated phrases, as does a public poster. Talking to a gathering of fans allows a dialogue of symbols and in-crowd semantics, as does an annual report to shareholders. All told, the tone of an illustration is shaped as much by the place it appears as the message it expresses.

International
Sushi Day
November 1, 2002

154

A day of fish. Each year on the first day of November, Japan celebrates Sushi Day. Following the annual rice harvest, this day is celebrated throughout the country, year after year.

I was asked to design a poster proclaiming the same day for the first time in the United States. Though far from a nationally recognized celebration, the day got its start in California.

I explored a few ideas with the actual food and even an origami fish, but felt that they lacked any sense of heritage and international reference. I decided to draw a Japanese woman reminiscent of the woodblock prints and paintings of the 1930s. The patterned design of the traditional kimono afforded me an opportunity to create the fish illusion and sushi reference.

I worked with a master Japanese calligrapher to create the lettering, and she also provided expert counsel on every detail of the clothing. I was assured that my final rendition was accurate; however, I was informed that my Japanese woman was clearly drawn by an American! The interpretation of the calligraphy roughly translates to "sushi is an internationally good food."

I opted for a less stylized typographic treatment in order to give the poster a more international feel. By placing the type flush left in the upper left-hand corner, the right corner was freed up to accommodate a downward-moving fish. The "s-like" flow of the fish added tremendously to the depth and composition of the finished poster.

155

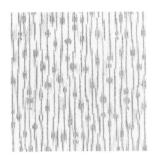

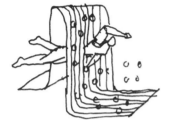

Surface treatment. The designer had a wonderful idea for bringing content and whimsy to the subtle distinctions of a collection of office floor coverings. For a catalog for Shaw Carpets, I was asked to do nine illustrations based on monochromatic watercolor renderings of each carpet's design. To add further intrigue, each carpet was given a name in the form of an interpretive phrase. "Without a care" is shown below, "Common sense" and the cover image "Green with envy," is on the opposite page.

Trading on the visual acuity of the catalog's audience, I was afforded great liberty in drawing these single-frame fantasies.

156

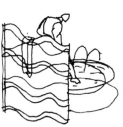

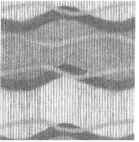

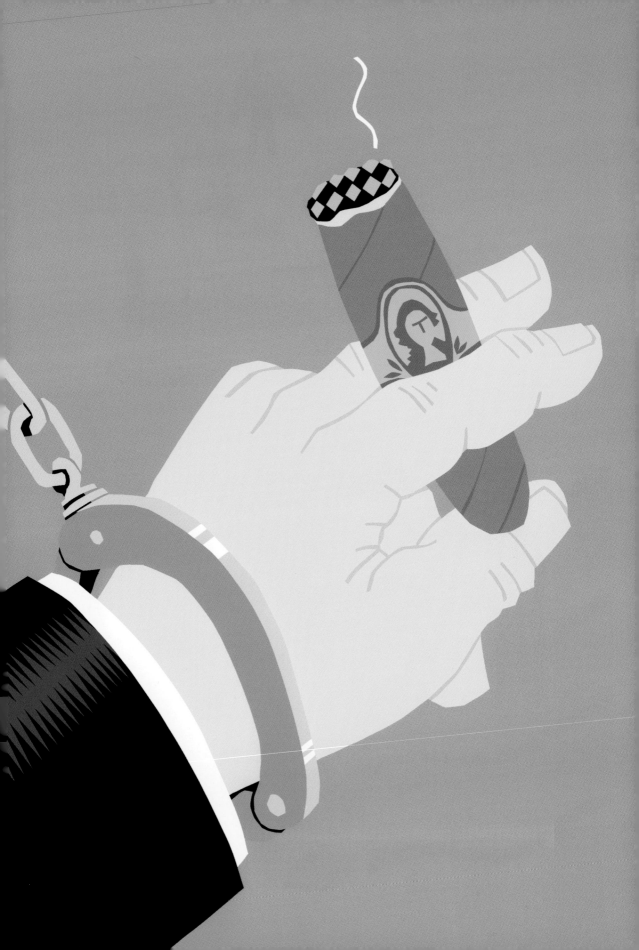

Taking account. In 2002, the financial world was rocked by the undoing of the stock market and the uncovering of several corporate accounting scandals. The public sentiment ranged from "where did all my money go?" to "lock the crooks away for life."

These subjects surfaced for me on several occasions in articles appearing in everything from international news magazines to university alumni publications. For an illustrator, the job is always a little more meaningful when you breathe the same air as the author. In

these cases, the illustrations tended to speak for the popular opinion, while at the same time offering up moderate doses of empathy and cynicism—both necessary in maintaining a balanced visual vocabulary .

159

Inside the box. The difficulty with corporate communications is that the outside view of a company is not always as unique as it appears from the inside. The designer's (and illustrator's) job is often to retell a story about the same virtues held by many other companies.

Some companies truly have a unique way of doing what would appear routine, and are willing to go further to express their difference.

This was a series used in an annual report for a young company that offers an automated stock trading service. The book thematically expressed the cultural aspects of the company and how they affect their daily business. A belief that what attracts their customers is their intrinsically smart value system.

It's a compelling approach, yet not automatically convincing. The key was that as smart as the company wanted to be portrayed, they wanted to grant that same intelligence to their shareholders. This suggested the tone I took.

I proposed that we show, in almost mechanical fashion, the simplicity of their messages.

They talked proudly about the new offices they built which positively affect the way they work, the idea of making a truly personal space—starting with a willingness to imagine what it could be. The illustration portrayed that idea in progress.

They talked about flexibility. Not in the traditional sense of bending over backward, but in the sense of readiness. The illustration revealed a shock-absorption system that is built for the rough road ahead.

All of the illustrations suggested a tone of voice—direct, engaging, and respectful.

160

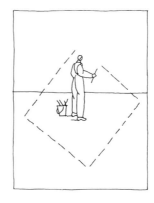
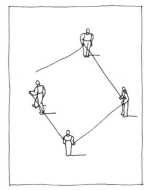

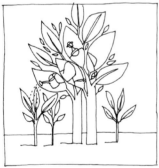

Inside job. This cover for the Orion Capital annual report illustrated what appeared, at first, as a typical corporate line. "Seeing beyond from within" actually presented an oxymoron that lent itself to an illusion. Implied in the message was that success breeds growth, which in turn creates an encumbrance. In this case, the company has turned the encumbrance into an asset.

In a "forest for the trees" mode, I explored the possible connections. I initially made fairly literal attempts at combining observation with the obstruction of trees. But there wasn't sufficient intrigue to make the idea unique.

Luckily, I saw the two trunk legs and drew the illusion from there. Without the figure in the tree leaves, the legs were only trunks. And without the legs, the figure had no basis for being in the tree. Thus making a magical interdependence with enough room for interpretation.

Voice. Tone.

Legal ease. Marketing lawyers is a difficult job at best. The inherent nature of their business defies the basic principle of promotion—selling. In fact, until the seventies, the profession didn't consider it an ethical practice to advertise at all.

I was approached by a lawyer friend about designing a promotional piece for his law firm. Concerned about what I could do for him, I was relieved to discover that he was a prolific writer and had published numerous editorials and articles on the profession. He was extremely outspoken about the degeneration of the profession and the lack of "civility" resulting from today's litigious society. His writings spoke volumes about his principles and beliefs—everything one would hope to put in a brochure about a company. Needless to say, this all made my decision to take the assignment easy.

My client selected and edited ten essays for publishing, five about what is wrong with lawyers and five about what is right with lawyers. I designed a book with two covers whose text opposed itself other by 180 degrees and then met in the middle.

I illustrated each essay with a simple black-and-white drawing and a short caption. Though not necessarily cartoons, my illustrations bore some resemblance to "*New Yorker*–style" lawyer jokes and looked quite comfortable within this context. Because the essays were quite serious, the illustrations offered a light and cynical punctuation to the author's views.

I think it must have been the honest and revealing nature of the content that made this assignment such a pleasure to work on.

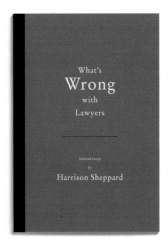

What's **Wrong** with Lawyers

Selected essays by

Harrison Sheppard

Harrison Sheppard *by* *Selected essays*

What's **Right** with Lawyers

Whether or not you have ever hired a lawyer, the behavior of lawyers is taking money out of your pocket. It is also putting you into a kind of prison without bars by making you more fearful about many ordinary human interactions. The character of much American lawyering has changed American life for the worse.

When I went to law school, I believed that being a lawyer was not only a good way to earn a living but a good way to live. It seemed to me then—as now—that the main purpose of being a lawyer is to help advance justice, peace, and human freedom. But law school was a shock to me. Not once in my three years of study was there a discussion of how a practicing lawyer can help advance these great ideals. Instead, law school taught me how to argue aggressively, with no quarter given or taken, and how to fight an opposing point of view with uncompromising technical skill. American law schools are exactly the kinds of institutions you would create if you wanted to promote a kind of civil war instead of civil peace. Law schools are not schools for

resolving conflict harmoniously; they are schools to help promote profitable conflict.

The lawyer as counselor, conciliator, problem-solver and planner used to be the model of the profession in this country. This model has been replaced by the gun for hire, the mercenary warrior. This is no longer merely irritating; in our highly individualistic, increasingly fragmented society, it has become downright dangerous. The tactics of litigating lawyers, in both civil and criminal matters, are causing the public to lose respect for our system of justice, the consequences are all too visible…

The most common defense aggressive lawyers make about their behavior is that they are doing what their clients have instructed them to do and are representing their clients' interests. This is often a self-serving defense for a lawyer's irresponsibility. It was answered a long time ago by a great American lawyer, Elihu Root, who said: "About half the practice of a decent lawyer consists in telling would-be clients that they are damned fools and should stop." It is, in other words, reason and humanity that should guide those who practice law. It is often natural for someone to

Cashing *in on* Conflict

Reprinted from *The Washington Post,* June 3, 1996

Politely preparing to negotiate the client's position.

seek legal advice with a desire for justice so excited that it amounts to vengeance. But every lawyer should want to serve his or her client's best interests. A hired gun only shoots bullets; what clients really need is the help of someone who can produce an outcome they can live with, even after anger has subsided, by resolving conflicts harmoniously…Helping to solve a client's problem with skillful counseling and negotiation is the kind of legal service most clients—particularly business clients—appreciate far more than costly, stressful litigation.

The character of American legal education needs to become a subject of serious national discussion. Law schools are the training grounds for our judges as well as our lawyers. They are not adequately providing students

with the skills they need to determine facts, understand a client's situation, counsel clients wisely, negotiate solutions and recognize the most practical, economical and stress-free means of resolving a client's situation.

The American legal profession and its most accomplished members have proven themselves to be among the most civilizing and progressive forces in history. American lawyers, going back at least to Thomas Jefferson, have helped to provide hope for a better life to all the world. To help increase the chance that our American future will be as bright as its promise, we need to do what we can to encourage restoration of the model of the American lawyer as a peacemaker.

"*Tell me a man is dishonest,
and I will answer he is no lawyer.
He cannot be, because the law is not in his heart,
is not the standard and rule of his conduct.*"
— Daniel Webster, 1847

Cynics believe there is nothing like a "moral economy" regulating the human enterprise. They cite as proof of their position, the fact that good people often suffer unjustly, while evil people often prosper. This apparently pragmatic view is dangerously short-sighted. It ignores the fact that in the great majority of cases, the truth is, in a sense, ruthless: sooner or later, it makes itself known.

Many lawyers show a Machiavellian contempt for truth. This is evident, for example, when lawyers attempt to destroy the credibility of witnesses who they know are telling the truth. There may be arguable justifications for this technique in certain criminal cases, where the State has the burden of proving its case "beyond a reasonable doubt." In civil cases, however, clients need to be wary of such lawyers, because their amorality may affect what they do when they perceive their own interests to conflict with their client's. Moreover, such amorality in court is not likely to serve the client's best interests. The discovery of risky lies told, or deceptions practiced, by the lawyer of a party to a lawsuit,

Lawyers who LIE

make matters worse for that party's side of the case than they would have been without them. While a client may be temporarily "rescued" by a lawyer's deceit, that client's life or enterprise may turn out to be poorer than it would have been if the truth had been disclosed in the light most sympathetic to the client. People are inclined to be forgiving when they are given reasons to forgive; and judges react more kindly to a wrong confessed than to a wrong concealed and discovered. This was once understood more widely by lawyers than it has been recently. Most lawyers today rely on tactics rather than prudent strategies grounded in the realities of a situation.

Clarence Darrow was one of the greatest lawyers of the early 20th century. He agreed to defend two wealthy Chicago youths who had committed a brutal murder for the "thrill" of it, Darrow didn't try to figure out what legal tricks he could play to prevent the DA from proving his clients were legally guilty. His greatest challenge was to save the boys' lives. So he pleaded them guilty, reserving the right to argue against the death penalty. He did this successfully, despite a widespread lynching attitude in

A lawyer presenting his own brand of the truth.

Chicago making it very difficult for the judge not to sentence his clients to death. Darrow succeeded by telling the truth about the circumstances of the crime, and the truth about the injustice, under Illinois law, of inflicting the death penalty on boys as young as his clients were. One of those clients, after serving his sentence of "life plus 99 years," lived to walk out of prison, write a book about his experiences, and spend the rest of his life with dignity, making significant contributions to medical science.

Lawyers who accept lying as part of their calling subvert the ends of justice and the judicial system. But this is not necessarily their

greatest wrong. "For true justice to be done," wrote the poet William Blake, "it must be done in minute particulars; justice in the abstract is the refuge of hypocrites and scoundrels." The worst thing about lawyers who lie may be that they don't give their own clients a chance to deal realistically with the honest truth, in service to their best interests. They thus deprive their clients of the opportunity to live their humanity most fully, denying them the profound grace and priceless gift of abiding by the sense of justice living in their own hearts.

12

13

165

Lawyers who know their respective areas of practice well, excel at keeping clients out of trouble. They also help clients avoid serious mistakes in horizons only lawyers are likely to see. "Knowing the law" means being able to identify the rules most relevant to a client's situation; how to find their latest form and interpretation; which courts have the authority to decide a particular dispute if it is litigated; and what the secourts' decisions are likely to be.

A good lawyer's ability to steer clients away from trouble and mistakes is the special stock in trade of business lawyers. Skillful drafting of a contract may not only help make the deal, it can help a client protect himself against a deal gone sour, and avoid its worst possible consequences. The skills of good commercial and contract lawyers, tax lawyers, corporate lawyers, securities lawyers, antitrust lawyers, and lawyers expert in other special fields of government regulation and administration, to take the most obvious examples, can make the difference between the success and failure of a business.

Most business lawyers are highly protective of their clients' interests. They are generally conservative in their judgments and try to identify all possible risks involved in a proposed course of action. Businessmen sometimes complain that their lawyers are better at telling them what they cannot do than what they can do, or how they can safely

Lawyers Who Know the Law *and Keep You Out of Trouble*

do what they want to do despite the risks. This conservatism, when sensibly understood by the client is, however, one of the things that is right with lawyers. A businessman who knows all the significant risks of a proposed course of action has an advantage over those who don't. If he is also able to make sound judgments about the degrees of risk involved, and the most likely consequences of taking them, he will be in the best possible position to decide the balance to be struck between risk and opportunity. To take a common example, it is ultimately for the client to decide whether a contract should address every possible risk the lawyer sees, or whether a deal and the relationship of the parties are such that a simple contract limited to the essential is the better option. The same kind of conservatism helps people avoid serious mistakes in their personal affairs, such as in the drafting of a will or the creation of a private trust. These documents are governed by a multitude of legal rules, and lawyers who know them well can help ensure that the document has the effects the client wants it to have, and not have unrealistic unforeseen and undesirable consequences.

Lawyers who are competent in their fields thus help clients foresee the probable and possible effects of what they aim to do, how they can do it in a way that best carries out their intentions, and, of course, how they can achieve their goals in compliance with the law.

A lawyer uncovering an optional course of action.

10

11

Keeping in tune. Santa Cruz Guitar Company is one of the last production manufacturers of handmade guitars. Staffed with some of the finest luthiers in the trade, the company makes instruments to order for some of the most discriminating guitar players in the world.

Having designed a photographic poster for Santa Cruz Guitars ten years previously, I was invited to design a limited-edition, illustrated version this time. If they were not as highly respected by both their fans and peers, I might have stuck with the traditional photograph, but their reputation called for something more esoteric.

Because their guitars are as beautiful to look at as they are to play, I decided to respond specifically to the lines and forms of the instruments. The musical qualities would simply have to be experienced in person. I looked briefly at casting the guitar with a supporting character like a woman or an Eames chair, but immediately felt that I was creating a distracton. The guitar needed to be center stage.

As happens quite often in sketching, I discovered an opportunity for creating a subtle illusion. If I made the guitar body the same color as the ground and didn't define its entire shape, I could pose the visual question, "is there a guitar there, or merely a guitar-shaped hole in the sky?" With that scenario established, I was free to weave a California Poppy behind the sky and out the through the side of the guitar's neck. I initially drew a bird circling in the sky but felt that it looked too contrived, so I removed it.

Handmade in the Northern California beach town of Santa Cruz, famous for its sunsets and Bohemian residents, these guitars come from a place like no other.

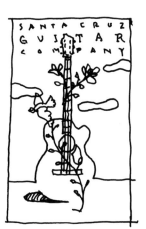

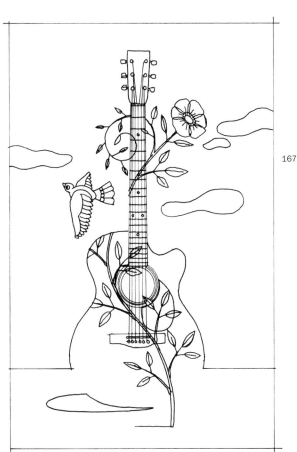

167

Beachfront property. For the first and last issue of the fashion magazine *Wink*, I was asked to illustrate an exposé about the male gigolo craze in the Dominican Republic.

Both the article and the fashion genre made the assignment attractive.

The story follows two characters, male and female, and their encounters on the island. The lure of the beach life and its trappings are central themes: surf, sand, and sex.

I proposed two sketches that were accepted right away. The theme of both was each character alone on the beach with the other character—larger than—life intersecting the scene. Less about a concept and more about a feeling.

The final illustrations were exercises in line and form, figure and ground, scale and contrast. The perceptual goal of each drawing was to make you toggle back and forth in your own mind between the two worlds. Each was dependent on the other, kind of like the story.

168

Fleeting moment. With a line like "dream without expectations," the assignment was uncomfortably wide open. This was an illustration for Sappi Fine Papers that appeared in advertising and brochures.

With the word "dream" in the headline, I was cautious not to state the obvious and draw something too esoteric. In fact, considering the audience of designers, I thought that it should be more concrete—

even suggestive—of creating something. "Without expectations" felt like a surprise should take place. Like stumbling onto a great idea.

I doodled around with a figure and his relationship to the horizon and to objects in nature. But nothing was simple enough. I wanted the illustration to portray a sense of transformation in an elementary way, like when dreams and ideas become something real.

Or when something real becomes a dream.

I love clouds. They define the sky, they are usually white, and they come in all shapes and sizes. They are puffy and lighter than air. They remind us of objects and transport our minds. They symbolize big ideas on the move.

I thought of the similarity between clouds and bubbles; both are dreamy and fleeting. The classic bubble blower was

a perfect symbol for the elementary mechanism—a contrast in scale and form from the clouds.

At this point, the drawing was purely a graphic exercise. I added the bucket to indicate his reservoir of thoughts and removed a cloud-like section of his body—the final expression of how deeply committed he was to his dream.

171

Speaking. Saying something. As communicators, we have to ask ourselves at the onset of an assignment, "do I have anything to offer here?" And at the end of the assignment ask again, "did I offer anything here?"

In order to answer yes to the first question, one has to have confidence that the answer to the second question will also be yes. Arriving at different answers with any degree of regularity prompts a thorough examination of everything we do. "Offering something here" is the name of the game.

To have a voice in every illustration one creates is often accomplished against great odds in today's design business. Our work is most often only a facet of someone else's "grand plan". And to only express our voice on occasions "when the situation is right" serves to never truly foster that voice. To shape our work to exclusively fulfill the plans of others is to risk not having a grand plan of our own.

To determinedly "put something personal" into every drawing we do is not selfish or adversarial, but rather committed and accountable. Tempering one's participation in the idea arena is short-selling the very role of the illustration, and drawing the blinds on the job of moving a reader's mind. The pursuit of "offering something here" is a tenet that never tires and never fails to elevate the meaning of "satisfying work".

If I had known what I know now. If I could do many of my earlier₁₇₅ assignments over they would be different. They would be easier, they would be executed more confidently, they would be funnier. But if that was the case, my work today would be different as well.

It seems that I am most influenced by the work completed yesterday. Maybe because it's the freshest and the closest to the surface of my mind. But I can't help my curiousity about the older work, more buried in my unconsciousness, and the role it plays in the big picture.

It's only in the course of doing this book that a thorough uncovering takes place. It is very difficult to look at the older work without imposing one's most current standards. But that hardly seems fair, given what I knew then. Needless to say, there was a great deal of work that survived the scrutiny and a fair bit that didn't make the cut. Mostly there was a recollection of the mistakes made, that became the lessons learned, that became the habits practiced, that became the work.

—Craig Frazier

I extend my gratitude to all
of the clients who have trusted
me and my work. It has been
my pleasure.